Contents

Introduction

This publication is designed to offer a **resource bank** of ideas for busy teachers to help them provide a range of reflective, participatory activities for pupils in **Religious Education** (RE) and through **collective worship** (especially class-based).

The approaches used here are also applicable across **other curriculum areas** depending on the stimuli chosen – e.g. in **History** (entering into the lived experience of someone from the past) or in **English** (considering the choices a character in a story has and how these might affect its plot).

There are also links with the **PSHE** and **Citizenship** aspects of the curriculum, particularly by helping pupils to think about their own experiences and tackling relevant spiritual and moral issues in reflective and empathetic ways. **Circle time**, both in primary and in the increasing number of secondary schools where this approach is used, would benefit from having some of these reflections form the basis for consideration.

The outlines are non-age-specific and as such the teacher needs to use their own judgement in adapting them for their age and ability grouping.

Religious Education – 'learning about' and 'learning from'

The terminology of RE being concerned with both 'learning about religions' and 'learning from religion' is now wide-spread across England and Wales and understood in Scotland and Northern Ireland. Many English Locally Agreed Syllabuses use these two 'attainment targets' as organising principles, drawing on the work done by the Qualifications and Curriculum Authority (QCA – non-statutory guidance, 2002) and its predecessor, the Schools Curriculum and Assessment Authority (SCAA – model syllabuses 1994).

Learning about religions has as its principal focus the content of the subject area in terms of developing knowledge and understanding of beliefs and practices and how these are reflected in the day-to-day life of believers.

Learning from religion is in essence about the application of that knowledge and understanding to the lives of the pupils and students. In other words, it is about asking the 'so what' question. Many Christians worship in a church, many Muslims in a mosque – so what? What does that mean for me – I don't worship anywhere? Sikhs believe in equality and show that through the *langar* – so what? What can I learn about equality from Sikhs when I don't know any?

Quality **Religious Education** is concerned with making sure that the balance is right between 'learning about' and 'learning from' with regard to both the content of the curriculum and the teaching and learning experiences provided for pupils and students.

Learning about religions

Knowledge and understanding

Content and factual detail

Quality Religious Education is about...

Balancing 'learning about' and 'learning from'

Learning from religion

Application

Affective

Relevant and personal

Spiritual and Moral Development

Spiritual

- awareness of and reflection on non-physical aspects of life – self, others, world, God (for many);
- application in terms of values and beliefs;
- creative, aesthetic, responsive, relational.

Spiritual

↓

all pupils – not confined to those with religious beliefs or of a particular faith

↓

fundamental to the human condition

↓

relationships – self, others, God

↓

search for individual and corporate identity

↓

response to experiences of life

↓

search for meaning and purpose and values by which to live

Moral

- understanding of principles of right and wrong and a willingness to act on them;
- personal, relational, societal, responsive.

Moral

↓

will to behave morally as a point of principle

↓

knowledge of codes of conduct agreed by society – what is considered to be right and wrong, and how do you know?

↓

understanding of how to make judgements on moral issues – personal and wider social issues

'**Education** is not only about seeking to promote high academic standards, but is also concerned with the all-round personal development of those engaged in the educational process – the one should complement and support the other. Ofsted recognises this when it gives high priority to focusing on the quality of the spiritual, moral, social and cultural development opportunities provided by the school and on the range of response to such provision by the pupils.'

Active learning

> **Active learning** is learning that involves pupils in **doing** things and **thinking** about (and consequently **learning from**) the things that they are doing.

'Learning by doing' is a theme that many educators have stressed since John Dewey argued in the 1930's that children must be engaged in an active quest for learning and new ideas. As Jean Piaget has said, 'knowledge arises neither from objects nor the child but from interactions between the child and the objects.'

'Active' does not always mean 'busy' learning – the reflective stimulus material and approaches outlined here are truly active in that they bring the 'object' into close 'interaction with the child'.

Thinking skills

The best RE has always encouraged pupils to think for themselves and to consider their own responses to issues of religious, spiritual and moral significance. The relatively recent emphasis on 'thinking skills' brought to the fore in England through the teaching and learning in the foundation subjects strand of the Key Stage 3 strategy reflects some of the excellent work that has been going on in classrooms and seeks to share that practice more widely.

What is new here for many who are teaching RE, both primary and secondary, is the element of metacognition – of encouraging pupils to 'think about their thinking' (the process of their thinking) in order to improve thinking and raise standards further.

The kinds of reflective activities outlined in this publication and their suggested follow-up activities can be enhanced further by encouraging pupils to consider how the experience or reflection they have been through helped them to assess issues, come to conclusions and revise their thinking.

Skill and attitude development

Planning to provide a wide range of reflective experiences can encourage pupils to develop the necessary skills and attitudes to aid them in their learning and is also an important tool in raising standards of achievement further. The experiences and reflections outlined here contribute to such skill and attitude development, especially:

Skills:

- **Interpretation** – understanding meaning or symbolism, religious language, suggesting meaning.
- **Reflection** – feelings, relationships, experience, ultimate questions, beliefs and practices.
- **Empathy** – consideration (thoughts, feelings, experiences, attitudes, beliefs and values) of others, imagination and identification (feelings such as love, wonder, forgiveness and sorrow), seeing through another's eyes.
- **Synthesis** – linking features of religion together into a coherent pattern, connecting different aspects of life.
- **Application** – making associations (religions, individual, community, national, international).
- **Expression** – explanation (concepts, rituals, practices), identifying and articulating matters of conviction and concern, responding to religious issues.

Attitudes:

- **Respect** – for self and others, recognising and respecting views, beliefs and customs of others, discerning between what is worthy of respect and what is not.
- **Self-understanding** – mature sense of self-worth and value, personal relevance of religious questions (and answers).

Guidelines for using guided visualisation and guided story in RE

Before

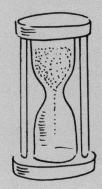

Negotiate ground rules. When using guided visualisation and guided story for the first time with pupils, ask for co-operation and invite them to share responsibility for what happens.

Start small. Pupils won't be able to participate in an extended activity straight away, so plan for around 10 minutes, and build on this.

Create the right atmosphere. Consider the following: How should pupils be seated or placed for the chosen activity? Would it be helpful to close the blinds? Should there be music playing in the background? Would a lighted candle or flower arrangement provide a useful focal point?

Plan B. Have an alternative activity ready in case things don't go to plan.

During

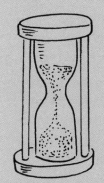

Be confident. Start in a clear, reassuring way, making sure that pupils know what is expected of them. Speak calmly and don't forget to allow appropriate pauses in the narrative. Welcome silence.

Stilling. Begin with a stilling exercise. Initially, select from the examples on pages 6 and 7.

Observing. Allow for non-active participation. A pupil can be invited to take the role of observer, without disturbing the others in the group.

Time. Keep an eye on the time; allow plenty of time for debriefing and follow-up.

Finishing. Finish by inviting pupils to rejoin the group, for example: 'When you are ready ... look up (or open your eyes) ... stretch if you want to ... Still ... be calm...'

Silence. Discourage talking immediately following the activity. Let there be a short pause, a moment of silence.

After

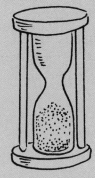

Follow-up. The follow-up activity or activities need to be planned carefully, and allow some choice either in the activity itself, or in the means by which it is expressed. Examples are provided for each exercise in the publication.

Sharing. Pupils should be given the opportunity to share their thoughts, feelings and experience in full-class discussion if they wish, but this should not be required, as personally sensitive issues may have been raised through the activity .

Debriefing. Follow-up discussion (paired, small group or whole-class) should ensure that pupils are:

- given adequate time to share ideas, thoughts and feelings;
- encouraged to listen carefully and sensitively to the ideas, thoughts and feelings of others;
- helped to articulate their learning through the experience.

Learning to be still ... preparing to reflect

Introduction

Sitting still, relaxing and preparing the body and mind to focus and reflect are skills that need to be learned. As much care and attention is needed here as for the lesson's main activity and follow-up.

Here you will find four suggestions to choose from to prepare pupils to take part in any of the activities outlined in this book. Each can be expanded and adapted according to the age and experience of the group, and the time available.

Each exercise has been set out as a script or framework. With experience, teachers will develop their own style and vocabulary.

Learning to sit still

→ Place your chair so that it is facing me and not touching your table...

→ Sit right back on your chair so that your back is right up against the back of the chair...

→ Put both feet flat on the floor...

→ Place your hands in your lap or let them lie loosely on your knees or on the table in front of you...

→ Give your shoulders a shrug to make sure you're relaxed even though you're sitting upright...

→ Now you're sitting in an alert relaxed position.

A variation

It may be possible for pupils to lie on the floor (preferably carpeted) for this exercise.

Breathing to relax

→ Now that you're sitting in an alert relaxed position, let your eyes close gently... (or look at the floor if you prefer ... so as not to distract others)...

→ Breathe slowly and silently ... noticing the way your breath enters and leaves your body ...

→ As you breathe in ... begin counting (in your mind) ... each time you breathe in, count to four ... one .... two ... three ... four...

→ Each time you breathe out, count to four ... one ... two ... three ... four ... and then start again...

→ If your mind wanders, bring it back gently and start from one again...

→ *(Pause for a short while, building up to perhaps a couple of minutes.)*

A variation

Ask pupils to imagine that as they breathe out, any tensions and worries they may have are breathed out. As they breathe in, things which are pleasant, comforting, and energising are breathed in.

Note

Pupils with breathing-related problems such as asthma or hayfever may find this activity difficult. An opportunity to observe should be provided.

Tensing

→ Now that you're sitting in an alert relaxed position ... let your eyes close gently (or look at the floor if you prefer, so as not to distract others)...

→ I'm going to ask you to focus on your body ... as I mention each part of your body ... feet ... hands ... face ... and so on ... I would like you to focus on that part...

→ First of all I want you to focus on your feet ... how do they feel? ... flex your toes ... and then let them relax...

→ Now do the same with the muscles in your legs ... tighten the muscles ... hold that tension for a moment ... and then let the muscles relax...

→ Lead pupils, in the same way, to focus on other parts of their body ... their bottom ... stomach ... chest ... shoulders ...neck ... different parts of the face ... scalp...

→ Pause for a short while, perhaps around a minute.

Note

The exercise can end here, or pupils can be led on to focus on their breathing as outlined in exercise 2 above, 'Breathing to relax'.

Using images

→ Now that you're sitting in an alert relaxed position ... let your eyes close gently (or look at the floor if you prefer, so as not to distract others)...

→ Imagine that you are in a favourite place ... somewhere you feel safe in ... relaxed ... calm ... it may be somewhere you know ... or it may be somewhere you have seen on the television or in photographs ... in your imagination spend a few moments looking around this place ... familiarise yourself with it...

→ Look closely ... what do you see? ... notice the colours ... shapes ... textures ... what can you hear? ... what is happening around you? ... are you alone or are there others? ... how do you feel? ... what are you thinking? ... spend a few moments enjoying your time in this special place ...

→ When you are ready ... slowly look up [open your eyes] ... come back into this room ... stretch if you want to ... rejoin the group ... Still ... be calm.

Variations

Pupils can be invited to choose their favourite place (as here) or the teacher can suggest a place (a lake, a beach, a park etc.) and invite pupils to imagine the details.

Questions

Let pupils share their responses in twos or threes, or as a class. Questions such as those below might be useful to focus the discussion.

- How did the exercise make you feel?
- What did it make you think about?
- Was there anything you liked or disliked about the exercise?
- Was there anything you found easy? Did you find anything hard?
- Did anything surprise you?
- How do you feel now?

Follow-up can also be in terms of artistic expression, e.g. using colours to explore feelings, or a drawing of their 'safe place'.

Beads

Suggested themes

Completion

Concentration

Duration

Existence

Meditation

Prayer

Reflection

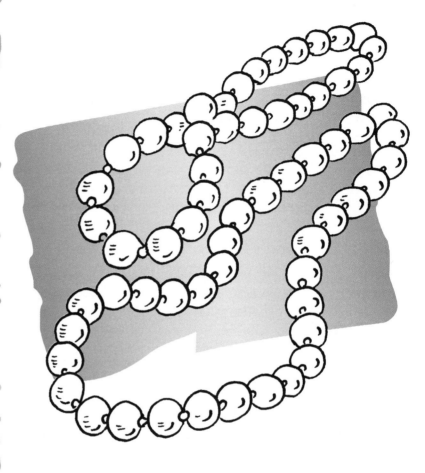

Equipment

- A simple string of beads (alternatively, a string of beads for each individual).
- Recording of prayers being said or chanted (see resources page).

What to do

→ Sit in a circle in a room where the lighting is soft.

→ Place the string of beads in the centre of the group where it is visible to everyone. Ask the group to look at the string of beads, to imagine and to note their feelings and ideas.

→ After a few minutes, remove the string of beads and play the recording of prayer being said or chanted. After a few minutes, replace the string of beads with the chant still being played. Allow time for individuals to note down their ideas.

→ Let pupils share their responses in twos or threes, and then follow this up by a general discussion of the interpretations, feelings and questions which the symbol arouses.

Questions

- What did the string of beads represent alone? Try and say why.
- What did the sound recording suggest to you?
- When the string of beads was replaced after the recording, had its meaning changed for you? If so, how?
- What special qualities do you think a string of beads has?
- How might you use a string of beads?

Follow-up work

Creativity

→ **Draw, paint or write a poem** to represent personal experience and feelings, expressing what the symbol meant personally.

→ **Compose a prayer or meditation** which could be said by someone thankful for the good things of life, or someone who isn't sure about belief in God.

Investigation and interpretation

→ Individually or in pairs, choose one of the main world religions from the course of study. Investigate and report on the place and symbolic meaning of prayer beads (or their alternatives, e.g. in Judaism) in the chosen religion.

Multi-faith examples

Supporting prayer: monks carry a rosary of 108 beads made of wood from the sacred bodhi tree. 108 corresponds to the number of sinful desires that the devotee must overcome in order to reach nirvana, and the number of Brahmins present at the Buddha's name-giving.

Supporting prayer: Christians may use a rosary to help them meditate on the key events in Jesus' life. Lay people use a rosary of five sets of ten beads separated by single larger beads with a crucifix on a set of four beads. A full rosary has 165 beads.

Supporting prayer: Hindus use a string of beads called a *mala*. Each bead represents a Hindu god or a prayer. Shiva's followers use a mala with thirty-two or sixty-four berries of the rudraksha tree. Vishnu's followers use one with 108 beads of tulsi wood. Swaminarayan Hindus use a kanthi.

Supporting prayer: Muslims use a string of beads called a *subha*. This is a ninety-nine-bead strand, divided into thirty-three-bead sections by marker beads. Each bead represents one of the ninety-nine names of Allah. The hundredth name can only be known in Paradise.

Supporting prayer: Judaism rejects rosaries because of their talismanic connections. To help them focus on prayer Jewish males use: a *tallit* (prayer shawl); *tefillin* (boxes containing text from Torah); a *kippah* or *yamulkah* (head covering).

Supporting prayer: Sikhs use a string of beads called a *mala*. These are usually made of a woollen cord which has 108 knots. They are used during personal devotions to help the devotee focus on God, so that God's qualities take root in the devotee.

Bell

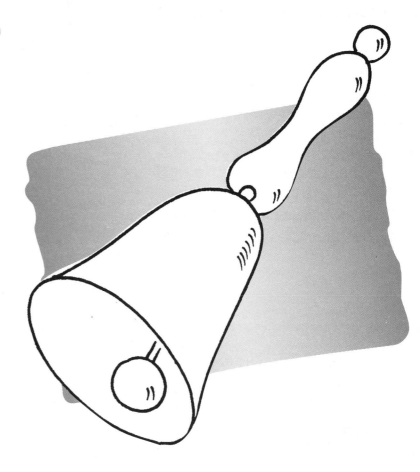

Suggested themes

Attracting attention

Beginnings

Calling

Places of worship

Prayer

Ritual or Liturgy

Sound

Equipment

- A small hand bell
- Tape or CD player
- Sounds of bells to play

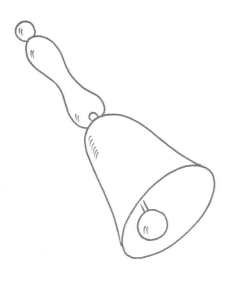

What to do

→ Sit in a circle in a room where the lighting is soft.

→ Place the bell in the centre of the group, on a table where it is visible to everyone. Ask the group to look at it while the recording is being played, to allow thoughts and associations to flow through their minds and to note their feelings and ideas.

→ After five minutes, remove the bell and stop the music. Allow time for individuals to note down their ideas.

→ Let pupils share their responses in twos or threes, and then follow this up by a general discussion of the interpretations, feelings and questions which the symbol arouses.

Questions

- What did the bell represent to you? Try and say why.
- What associations did it bring to mind?
- What other kinds of bells are there? What are their functions?
- What qualities does the sound of a bell have?
- What past or current events did the bell bring to mind?

Follow-up work

Creativity

→ **Draw, paint or write a poem** to represent personal experience and feelings, expressing what the symbol meant personally.

→ **Compose music** exploring themes of 'calling', 'declaring' and 'awakening'.

→ **Create a festival of sound.** Choose its significance, design a ceremony, select an occasion when it can be shared and present the idea to an audience (e.g. collective worship).

Investigation and interpretation

→ Individually or in pairs, choose one of the main world religions from the course of study. Investigate and report on the place and symbolic meaning of 'sound' in the chosen religion.

Multi-faith examples

Drawing attention: ringing a bell to attract the attention of the worshipper and to accompany the chanting of verses and mantras.

Symbolising wisdom: the hollow symbolises wisdom recognising emptiness; the clapper represents the sound of emptiness.
Marking significant moments: ringing the sanctus bell at the holiest part of the Eucharist; tolling of a bell after death; ringing a bell during a wedding service.
Calling people to worship: ringing a bell before Sunday services.

Drawing attention: ringing a bell to summon the god when entering the temple and to announce arrival.
Symbolising rank and dignity: when worn by Nandi the Bull, the vehicle of Shiva.

Summoning people to prayer: the *adhan* (call to prayer) is made five times a day, by the *mu'adhin* (muezzin).
Playing music: music is never used in worship; Muslims hold different views about whether it is ever acceptable or permitted.

Symbolising authority: worn as part of the ancient temple priest's vestments; attached to the Sefer Torah, as decoration.
Drawing attention: a *shofar* (ram's horn) is blown during the festival of Rosh Hashanah to arouse thoughts of repentance.

Assisting worship: using small bells to accompany the singing of *shabads* as part of worship. These are hymns outlined in the Guru Granth Sahib which express the qualities of God. They are also known as *Gurbani* (Message of the Teacher).

Book

Suggested themes

Holy books

Hope

Insight

Revelation

Truth

Understanding

Equipment

- An open book without written words or pictures (i.e. blank)
- A book stand (optional)
- Internet access (optional)

What to do

→ Sit in a circle in a room where the lighting is soft.

→ Place the book on the stand in the centre of the group, on a table where it is visible to everyone.

→ Ask the group to look at it and to allow thoughts and associations to flow through their minds and to note their feelings and ideas.

→ Tell pupils that it is now a book that is to be written about their whole lives, individually. Ask them to try to imagine themselves at the age of 70 looking back on their life.

→ What events, ideas and feelings do they think the book will contain?

→ Is there anything that they would like to change or remove?

→ What would they like to add?

→ How would they feel if the book were mistreated or destroyed?

→ After a few minutes, remove the book. Allow time for individuals to reflect and note down their ideas.

→ Let pupils share their responses in twos or threes. Then follow this up by a general discussion of the interpretations and feelings which the symbol aroused.

Questions

- What did the book represent to you? Try and say why.
- What association(s) did it bring to mind?
- What did you imagine the book would contain if it were your biography?
- What things did you wish you could change or remove? What things did you want to add?
- How did you feel about the book being mistreated or destroyed? Try and say why.

Follow-up work

Creativity

→ **Draw, paint or write a poem** to represent personal experience and feelings, expressing what the symbol meant personally.
→ **Compose an entry** for an internet biography collection on an inspirational person (200 words maximum).

Reflection

→ **Keep a reflective diary** for a week, on a theme such as 'Good things that happened to me', 'When I got angry', 'When I felt sad'.

Interpretation and application

→ Individually or in pairs, choose one of the main world religions from the course of study. Produce a list of advantages and disadvantages of the text being available on the internet. If internet access is possible, pupils could spend 10–15 minutes (no more) exploring how the sacred texts of the religion they have chosen is presented, and suggest who the target audience might be. See below for resources.

Multi-faith examples

Tripitaka, Dhammapada, Kalama Sutta and more: www.buddhanet.net
Dhammapada for children: www.buddhanet.net/frames47.htm

The Bible: http://bible.gospelcom.net/bible?
Audio Bible (King James version): www.audio-bible.com/bible

Vedas, Upanishads, Ramayana, Mahabharata and Bhagavad Gita: www.sacred-texts.com/hin
Daily Bhagavad Gita: www.geocities.com/Athens/Acropolis/5294

The Qur'an, Hadiths and other texts: www.ishwar.com
Qur'an recitations: www.islam.org

TeNaKh, Talmud, Hagadah and Midrash: www.sacred-texts.com/jud
Children's Torah portion: www.akhlah.com/parsha/parisha.asp

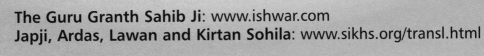

The Guru Granth Sahib Ji: www.ishwar.com
Japji, Ardas, Lawan and Kirtan Sohila: www.sikhs.org/transl.html

Bread

Suggested themes

Celebration

Equality

Eucharist

Gratitude

Life

Pesach

Service

Spiritual growth

Equipment

• A loaf of bread which has been cut with a knife
• A bread knife
• A candle

What to do

→ Sit in a circle in a room where the lighting is soft.

→ Place the loaf of bread in the centre of the group, on a table where it is visible to everyone. Ask the group to look at it and to allow thoughts and associations to flow through their minds and to note their feelings and ideas.

→ Place a candle alongside the loaf of bread and ask the pupils again to allow thoughts and associations to flow through their minds and to note their feelings and ideas.

→ Break the bread in enough pieces and ask members of the group to offer pieces to others in the circle, who then eat them. Again allow time for thought, and for pupils to note down their ideas.

→ Let pupils share their responses in twos or threes. Then follow this up by a general discussion of the interpretations and feelings which the exercise aroused.

Questions

- What did the loaf of bread represent to you? Try and say why.
- What association(s) did it bring to mind?
- What did you imagine when the bread was lit by a candle?
- What did you think about when you were offered some to eat?
- What did you think about when you ate the bread?

Follow-up work

Creativity

→ **Draw, paint or write a poem** to represent personal experience and feelings, expressing what the symbol meant personally.

→ **Compose a poem or story** to explore 'Bread, the food of life', or 'The last loaf of bread in the world'.

→ **Create a festival** involving bread. Choose a focus, design a ceremony, select an occasion when it can be shared and present the idea to an audience (e.g. collective worship).

Investigation and interpretation

→ Individually or in pairs, choose one of the main world religions from the course of study. Investigate and report on the place and symbolic meaning of bread in the chosen religion.

Multi-faith examples

Offering worship (*puja*): rice may be offered as an expression of gratitude or to involve the emotions in following the Buddhist path.
Showing generosity (*dana*): lay people provide monks and nuns with food, regarding it as a privilege and a source of merit.

Expressing beliefs: God as provider of material and spiritual needs; Jesus as the 'bread of life'; breaking of bread in the Eucharist as a symbol of Jesus' sacrificial death.
Expressing gratitude: Harvest festival.

Offering worship (*puja*): food offerings are made ceremonially to the deity to say thank you for the good things given.
Expressing God's blessing: serving *Prashad* (food which has been offered to the deity) to devotees after *puja*.

Expressing beliefs: eating only permitted food (*halal*); fasting during Ramadan (*sawm*).
Showing generosity: provision of food for the needy (animals slaughtered at Id-ul-Fitr); *Zakat*; *Zakat-ul-Fitr* (the poor-due at Id-ul-Fitr).

Expressing beliefs: eating only permitted food (kosher); understanding why *Matzah* is eaten at *Pesach*.
Thanking God: the *challot* (two loaves of plaited white bread) remind Jews of their dependence on God each Shabbat.

Expressing worship: the *langar* (kitchen) represents service to others, an important aspect of worship.
Symbolising equality: serving *Karah Parshad* at religious ceremonies in the presence of the Guru Granth.

Candle and barbed wire

Suggested themes

Crucifixion

Enlightenment

God

Hope

Justice

Life

Light

Suffering

Equipment

- A candle
- A candle holder (optional)
- Matches
- Spiral of barbed wire to fit around the candle
- Resources to record personal response (e.g. paper, coloured pens or pencils, ICT access)

What to do

→ Sit in a circle in a room where the lighting is soft.

→ The group should be used to reflective silence and be willing to sit quietly, and still, for some time.

→ Place a candle in the centre of the group, on a table where it is visible to everyone. Ask the group to look at the candle and speak out their responses to watching the flame (or write them down).

→ After a few minutes, take away the candle and put a spiral of barbed wire in its place. Again, ask the group to speak out (or write down) their feelings and responses.

→ After a few minutes, place the candle inside the spiral of wire (see illustration). Allow the group time to respond, as above.

→ Ask pupils to collect the resources they need to complete a personal response to the exercise (see suggestions). Then provide an opportunity for discussion, initially in twos and threes and then as a whole class.

→ A group activity can follow to develop understanding of themes or concepts raised (see suggestions).

Questions

- What did the candle alone represent to you?
- What did the barbed wire alone represent to you?
- What did the candle surrounded by the barbed wire represent to you?
- What did you feel most strongly when viewing each symbol?
- Do the symbols remind you of any past events or current events? What do they say about those events?

Follow-up work

Individual work (this could remain private)

→ **Draw, paint or write a poem** to represent personal experience and feelings, expressing what the symbol(s) meant personally. Responses can be to one or all parts of the symbol.

→ **Create a symbol** to represent the meaning identified most clearly or strongly in the activity.

Group work

→ **Prepare and present a dance or drama** expressing the different meanings and questions identified by the group.

→ **Investigation and interpretation:** Individually or in pairs, choose one of the main world religions from the course of study. Investigate and present how the meanings you have identified are understood in that religion (see suggestions below).

Multi-faith examples

Expressing understanding of suffering and how it might be overcome: the Four Noble Truths and the Noble Eightfold Path. **Representing a way of seeing and relating to life, free of hindrances and attachments:** i.e. Enlightenment.

Celebrating: festivals (e.g. Advent, Christmas, Easter) and times of personal commitment (e.g. baptism). **Expressing beliefs:** Jesus' crucifixion; Jesus as the 'light of the world'; disciple of Jesus as 'light in the world'; goodness overcoming evil; hope.

Celebrating festivals and telling stories about goodness being stronger than evil: Holi, Divali and Navaratri. **Representing through ritual action the desire to seek enlightenment:** the *arti* ceremony.

Suggesting an aspect of Allah: 'Allah is the light of the heavens and the earth ... Allah guides to His light whom He pleases.' Qur'an 24:35. **Struggling to overcome personal temptation:** greater *jihad*; stoning of pillars at Mina when on *Hajj*.

Symbolising God's presence and the light of the Torah: the *Ner Tamid* above the Ark; the festival of Hanukkah. **Reminding of key beliefs:** light is a gift from God the creator (e.g. Shabbat candles); and God sustains the faithful (e.g. the *Shoah*).

Representing essential teaching: the obligation to defend the truth and to try to live within God's rule (e.g. the *khanda*). **Living a life of service:** to God, the *khalsa* and to humanity in general (i.e. *sewa*).

Clock

Suggested themes

Cause and effect
Endurance
Fulfilment
Judgement
Life span
Marking time
Responsibility
Seasons

Equipment

• A clock, preferably with a loud tick

What to do

→ Sit in a circle in a room where the lighting is soft.

→ Place the clock in the centre of the group, on a table where it is visible to everyone. Ask the group to look at it and to allow thoughts and associations to flow through their minds and to note their feelings and ideas.

→ After a few minutes, remove the clock. Allow time for individuals to note down their ideas.

→ Let pupils share their responses in twos or threes, and then follow this up by a general discussion of the interpretations, feelings and questions which the symbol arouses.

Questions

- What did the clock represent to you? Try and say why.
- What association(s) did it bring to mind?
- Did time pass quickly or slowly during this exercise? Try and say why.
- What do you think about and feel when time passes slowly, and when it passes quickly?
- What things would you do if you had more time?

Follow-up work

Creativity

→ **Draw or paint** an expression of what 'time' means personally.

→ **Compose a poem or story** with the title 'Eternity', 'If I only had time' or 'Cause and effect'.

→ **Prepare and present a dance or drama** about the qualities and values involved in 'things done or said in haste' and 'things done too slowly'.

Reflection

→ **Keep a reflective diary** for a week, on a theme such as 'Time spent on myself, time spent on others, time other people spent on me'.

Multi-faith examples

 Expressing beliefs: time is cyclical; individual existence is believed to be a repeated sequence of birth, death, and rebirth as the soul seeks spiritual enlightenment; the lotus flower symbolises the simultaneousness of cause and effect.

 Expressing beliefs: time is linear; it is a God-given gift which should be wisely and responsibly used; the time of judgement will come when decisions can no longer be put off.
Using time: loving God, and loving neighbour.

 Expressing beliefs: time is cyclical; individual existence is believed to be a repeated sequence of birth, death, and rebirth as the soul seeks spiritual enlightenment; certain times are better than others for important events (marriage, business ventures, religious rites).

 Expressing beliefs: time is linear; it is a God-given gift which should be wisely and responsibly used.
Using time: setting aside time for prayer (*salah*) – the five required daily prayers (*fard*) and additional personal prayer (*du'a*).

 Expressing beliefs: time is linear; it is a God-given gift which should be wisely and responsibly used.
Marking events: through weekly and annual festivals and celebrations reflecting beliefs about identity, purpose and authority.

 Expressing beliefs: time is cyclical; individual existence is believed to be a repeated sequence of birth, death, and rebirth as the soul seeks spiritual enlightenment.
Using time: meditating on God's name; serving others (*sewa*).

Computer

Suggested themes

Communication

Discernment

Education

Knowledge

Learning

Understanding

Worship

Equipment

• A computer (showing the desktop or a search engine), with screen and keyboard visible

• Peripherals such as printer and scanner (optional)

What to do

➔ Sit in a semi-circle in a room where the lighting is soft, and where all can see a computer screen and keyboard.

➔ Ask the group to look at the computer and to allow thoughts and associations to flow through their minds and to note their feelings and ideas. Ask how computers affect their daily lives. How might this be similar or different for younger and older members of their family? What changes can they foresee over the next two or three years? What excites them, what concerns them?

➔ Tell pupils that it is now a computer that can answer any question they choose to ask.

➔ What questions would they like to ask the computer?

➔ What answers do they think they would receive?

➔ Are there any questions which it would be unwise for people to know the answer to? What might these questions be?

➔ After a few minutes, turn off the computer. Allow time for individuals to reflect and note down their ideas.

➔ Let pupils share their responses in twos or threes. Then follow this up by a general discussion of the interpretations and feelings which the symbol aroused.

Questions

- What did the computer represent to you? Try and say why.
- What association(s) did it bring to mind?
- What question did you ask the computer to answer? What reply did you receive?
- Are there any questions which it is better for humans not to know the answer to?
- What ideas did you have about how computers should be used?

Follow-up work

Creativity

→**Draw, paint, or write a poem** to represent how lives in the future will be influenced by computer technology, and personal feelings about this.

→**Compose a piece of extended writing** called 'The computer which knows everything' or 'A day in the life of a computer'.

Analysis and expression

→**Individually** or in pairs, choose one of the main world religions from the course of study. Analyse and write a review (200 words maximum) of one of the websites listed. The review is for a magazine read by teenage members of the religion chosen.

Multi-faith examples

Worship: www.buddhamind.info (select 'shrine room')
Information and community: www.buddhanet.net

Worship: www.embody.co.uk and www.visions-york.org
Information and community: http://rejesus.co.uk

Worship: www.archaka.com
Information and community: www.indiadivine.com and www.swaminarayan.org

Worship: www.islamicity.com
Information and community: www.islam.org (Sunni) and www.al-islam.org (Shi'a)

Worship: www.thinkjewish.com/walk.html
Information and community: www.virtualjerusalem.com

Worship: www.sgpc.net/hukumnama
Information and community: www.panthkhalsa.org and www.sikhkids.com

Egg

Suggested themes

Beginnings

Birth

Creation

New life

Potential

Rebirth

Equipment

- An egg, on a stand which does not obscure full view

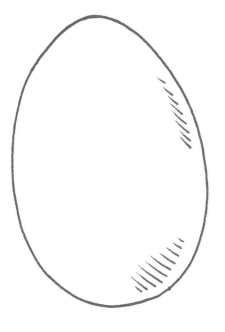

What to do

→ Sit in a circle in a room where the lighting is soft.

→ The group should be used to reflective silence and willing to sit quietly, and still, for some time.

→ Place the egg in the centre of this group, on a table where it is visible to everyone. Ask the group to look at the egg and try to imagine what it must feel like to be inside it, and to break out of it. Ask the group to keep a note of their feelings and ideas whilst looking and imagining.

→ After five minutes, take the egg away. Allow time for individuals to note down their ideas.

→ Share ideas first in twos and threes and later as a whole class. This should include a general discussion of the interpretations and feelings which the symbol aroused.

Questions

- What did the egg represent to you? Try and say why.
- What memories and associations did it bring to your mind?
- What did you think that life inside an egg would be like?
- What feelings did you experience while imagining what it would be like to be inside?
- What past or current events did it bring to mind? What does it say about these events?

Follow-up work

Creativity

→ **Design a decorated egg** expressing what the symbol meant personally.

→ **Draw, paint or write a poem** to represent 'Existence inside an egg'.

→ **Plan and present a dance or drama** expressing ideas of rebirth or new beginning(s).

→ **Investigation and interpretation:** Individually or in pairs, choose one of the main world religions from the course of study. Investigate and report on the place and symbolic meaning of the egg in the chosen religion.

Multi-faith examples

 Expressing beliefs: the first of the Five Precepts is to refrain from destroying living creatures; many practising Buddhists are vegetarian and some are vegan; abortion is generally to be avoided but may be permitted for compassionate reasons.

 Expressing beliefs: dyed red or painted (Jesus' resurrection, the stone rolled away from the tomb); Easter eggs (symbol of fertility, new life and hope); abortion is generally to be avoided but may be permitted for compassionate reasons (e.g. rape) by some Christians.

 Expressing beliefs: the first act of creation is described as an egg breaking in two (Upanishads); life begins at the moment the egg is fertilised (conception); abortion may be permitted by Hindus depending on circumstances, and the law of the country concerned.

 Expressing beliefs: symbol of fertility; life begins at the moment the egg is fertilised (conception); abortion is generally to be avoided but is permitted to save the life of the mother and (by some Muslims) if there is risk of serious deformity or disease.

 Expressing beliefs: the roasted egg, symbol of sacrifice in the Temple, and placed on the Passover plate; life begins at the moment the egg is fertilised (conception); abortion is generally to be avoided but is permitted by some Jews to save the life of the mother, or in cases of rape.

 Expressing beliefs: symbol of fertility; life begins at the moment the egg is fertilised (conception) and is in God's hands; abortion is generally to be avoided but may be permitted by some Sikhs in serious circumstances such as rape.

Flowers

Suggested themes

Beauty

Celebration

Creation

Death

Festivity

Growth

Life

Source

Equipment

- Flowers in a vase – several varieties, alive
- A few dead flowers

What to do

→ Sit in a circle in a room where the lighting is soft.

→ First, place the vase of living flowers in the centre of the group, on a table where it is visible to everyone. Ask the group to look at it and to allow thoughts and associations to flow through their minds and to note their feelings and ideas. After a few minutes, replace the vase of living flowers with some withered flowers, scattered on the table.

→ After a few minutes, remove the flowers. Allow time for individuals to note down their ideas.

→ Let pupils share their responses in twos or threes, and then follow this up by a general discussion of the interpretations, feelings and questions which the symbol arouses.

Questions

- What did the two sets of flowers represent to you? Try and say why.
- What association(s) did they bring to mind?
- What special qualities do flowers have?
- What past or current events did the experience bring to mind?
- How might your ideas be different if artificial flowers had been used? Or dried flowers?

Follow-up work

Creativity

→ **Draw, paint or write a poem** to represent personal experience and feelings, expressing what the symbol meant personally.

→ **Design a collage of flowers** on a chosen theme, e.g. 'harmony', 'celebration' or 'life and death'.

→ **Create a festival involving flowers**. Choose its significance, design a ceremony, select an occasion when it can be shared and present the idea to an audience (e.g. collective worship).

Investigation and interpretation

→ Individually or in pairs, choose one of the main world religions from the course of study. Investigate and report on the place and symbolic meaning of flowers in the chosen religion.

Multi-faith examples

Expressing belief: offered to statues of Buddha as an act of worship; the lotus flower is sacred to Buddha who is viewed as the flame of the sacred fire coming from the centre of the lotus flower; represents time, creation, peace and harmony.

Expressing belief: the lily represents purity, chastity and innocence as it flowers from what seems a lifeless bulb (symbol of resurrection and Easter); the rose represents the blood of Christ, and sorrow, and is a symbol of mystical and spiritual love.

Expressing belief: flowers are offered in temples and shrines as an act of worship; a bride and groom exchange garlands in the wedding ceremony; thrown onto the Ganges when the ashes of the dead are sprinkled; Brahma and Lakshmi sprang from the lotus flower.

Expressing belief: the rose is a sacred plant that springs from the drops of perspiration of the prophet during his night journey; rose water is used to wash the Ka'ba before *Hajj*; abstract designs taken from the flower shapes are used to ornament mosques and buildings.

Expressing belief: flowers are rarely seen on graves in traditional Jewish cemeteries (stones are used instead, piled without pattern on the grave); plant images are widely used in Jewish art and life in general.

Expressing belief: the parents of a bride welcome the groom and his parents and garland them with flowers; the bride garlands the groom, and receives a garland in return; some Sikhs place the dead in a coffin ornamented with flowers and wreaths.

Fruit

Suggested themes

Evil

Fertility

Immortality

Knowledge

Life

Readiness

Temptation

Equipment

- A bowl of different kinds of fruit (apples, oranges, bananas, grapes etc)
- An apple with a large bite taken out of it

What to do

→ Sit in a circle in a room where the lighting is soft.

→ Place the bowl of fruit in the centre of the group, on a table where it is visible to everyone. Ask the group to look at it and to allow thoughts and associations to flow through their minds and to note their feelings and ideas.

→ After a few moments, replace the bowl of fruit with a single apple that has one bite taken out of it. Ask pupils to look at it and allow thoughts and associations to flow through their minds and note their feelings and ideas.

→ After a few moments, remove the apple. Allow time for individuals to note down their ideas.

→ Let pupils share their responses in twos or threes, and then follow this up by a general discussion of the interpretations, feelings and questions which the symbols arouse.

Questions

- What did the bowl of fruit represent to you? Try and say why.
- What association(s) did it bring to mind?
- What did the apple alone represent to you? Try and say why.
- What association(s) did it bring to mind?

Follow-up work

Creativity

→ **Draw, paint or write a poem** to represent personal experience and feelings, expressing what the symbol meant personally.

Reflection

→ **Read and think about** the words below. Imagine that another type of fruit had been described. Choose the fruit, and then describe it in the way you think Brian Keenan might do.

Brian Keenan, a journalist, was abducted in Beirut and held hostage in appalling conditions. In his book *An evil cradling*, he describes his reaction to the unexpected appearance of a bowl of fruit:

'The fruits the colours, mesmerising me ... I am entranced by colour.... The colour orange, the colour, the colour, my God the colour orange... Such wonder ... such absolute wonder in such an insignificant fruit ... My soul finds its own completeness in the bowl of colour. The forms of each fruit. The shape and curl and bend are so rich, so perfect. I want to bow down before it, loving that blazing, roaring, orange colour.'

Multi-faith examples

Offering worship (*puja*): rice may be offered as an expression of gratitude or to involve the emotions in following the Buddhist path.
Showing generosity (*dana*): lay people provide monks and nuns with food, regarding it as a privilege and a source of merit.

Expressing beliefs: God as provider of material and spiritual needs; symbolic of salvation (Mary – new Eve; Christ – new Adam).
Explaining sin and temptation: the story of Adam and Eve in the Garden of Eden (Genesis 3); fruit of the tree of life.

Offering worship (*puja*): food offerings are made ceremonially to the deity to say thank you for the good things given.
Expressing God's blessing: serving *Prashad* (food which has been offered to the deity) to devotees after *puja*.

Expressing beliefs: eating only permitted food (*halal*); fasting during Ramadan (*sawm*).
Explaining sin and temptation: the story of Adam and Eve in Paradise (*Al-A'raf*).

Expressing beliefs: eating only permitted food (*kosher*); thanking God for providing food (festival of *Sukkot*).
Explaining sin and temptation: story of Adam and Eve in the Garden of Eden (Genesis 3); fruit of the tree of life.

Expressing worship: the *langar* (kitchen) represents service to others, an important aspect of worship.
Symbolising equality: serving *Karah Parshad* at religious ceremonies in the presence of the Guru Granth.

Hands

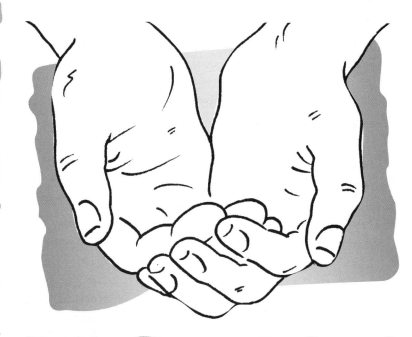

Suggested themes

Actions

Attitudes

Blessing

Communication

Meditation

Protection

Service

Values

Equipment

• None needed

What to do

➔ Sit in a circle in a room where the lighting is soft.

➔ Ask pupils first to choose one of their hands and to study it very carefully, concentrating on the shape of the fingers, the nails, the lines on the hand, the colour, any irregularities and so on, until they feel they know their hand very well.

➔ Ask pupils to note down any special qualities of their hand. Ask, 'What do you remember and think of when you look at your hand?'

➔ Ask pupils to place the palms of their hands on their knees and then think of all the things they most want to get rid of. These can be physical things or abstract qualities. As they do this exercise they should press the palms of their hands down on to their knees as a way of releasing these unwanted thoughts.

➔ Next pupils should turn the palms of their hands upwards and think of all the things they would wish to receive – again these can be physical objects or abstract qualities (encourage the latter).

➔ Let pupils share their responses in twos or threes. Then follow this up by a general discussion of the interpretations and feelings which the exercise aroused.

Questions

- What did you notice about your hand?
- What association(s) did it bring to mind?
- What special qualities did your hand have?
- What things did you want to get rid of?
- What things did you want to receive?
- How helpful did you find the use of hands in your thinking and imagining?

Follow-up work

Creativity

→ **Draw, paint or write a poem** to express what contemplating your hand meant personally.
→ **Compose a piece of extended writing** called 'A portrait of my hand' or 'A day in the life of my hand'.

Reflection

→ Using A4 paper, draw round a hand and cut out the shape. Write on it the thing you most want to receive. Tie everyone's shapes onto an old branch of wood, like leaves. This creates a tree of wishes (or prayers). [This activity can be adapted to a variety of situations, e.g. things pupils would wish to forget, lose, enjoy or achieve.]

Investigation and interpretation

→ Individually, or in pairs, choose one of the main world religions from the course of study. Investigate and make a presentation on the place and symbolic meaning of hands in the chosen religion (see suggestions below).

Multi-faith examples

 Expressing beliefs about Lord Buddha: the palm upwards (unlimited giving); the right hand touching the earth (his lordship over it); his left hand holding the alms bowl or turning upwards (receptivity and surrender).

 Expressing aspects of belief and practice: the hand of God (his power); a hand raised (God's blessing); shaking hands at worship (peace, love and friendship); laying on of hands at confirmation and ordination (symbolic transference of God's Spirit).

 **Expressing beliefs about Lord Shiva:** the hand raised (peace and protection); the hand lowered, pointing to the foot (deliverance); the drum beat (the creative act); the flame in the hand (the destruction of the world by fire).

 **Expressing aspects of belief and practice:** the open hand (blessing, adoration and hospitality); the Hand of Fatima (the hand of God, divine power, providence, generosity and healing). The hand also represents the five pillars of Islam.

Expressing aspects of belief and practice: the arm of God (God's power); Jewish woman waving hands over the Sabbath candles (welcoming in the Sabbath); hand-shaped *challah* (symbolic of the desire to be inscribed in the book of life).

 Expressing aspects of belief and practice: wearing a *kara* (steel band – one of the Five Ks and an outward sign of commitment); folding hands when standing in front of the Guru Granth (humility and respect); *sewa* (service to others).

Mirror

Suggested themes

Character

God

Insight

Perceptions

Reflections

Truth

Universe

Wisdom

Equipment

- A mirror for each person in the group

What to do

→ Sit in a circle in a room where the lighting is soft.

→ Each pupil needs to have a mirror. First, tell the pupils to look carefully in the mirror at their own reflection and to allow thoughts and associations to flow through their minds and to note their feelings and ideas.

→ Encourage students first to explore their own faces as a map, noting physical features etc. Then encourage them to think about abstract qualities and characteristics.

→ After a few minutes, ask the pupils to angle the mirror so that they can concentrate on one feature in the classroom or in the environment which can be seen in the mirror. Allow thoughts and associations to flow through their minds and to note feelings and ideas.

→ Let pupils share their responses in twos or threes. Then follow this up by a general discussion of the interpretations and feelings which the symbol aroused.

Questions

- What did you think about when looking at your own reflection? Try and say why.
- What did you think about when looking at something else?
- How did you feel when asked to look at your own reflection and think?
- How easy did you find it to share your ideas about yourself and others?
- What is different about viewing things in a mirror and viewing objects in reality?

Follow-up work

Creativity

→**Photography.** As a group, take a series of photographic images entitled 'Reflections' showing the world reflected in a variety of ways, and from a variety of perspectives: e.g. culture, religion, age or mood.
Sequence the images (e.g. using *PowerPoint* or similar software) and compose a title for each image. Music could be added.

→**Prepare and present a dance or drama** entitled 'The two-way mirror', exploring what can be seen through it and in it.

Reflection

→**Compose a drawing, painting or poem** to represent an aspect of your life which you are happy with, and an aspect of your life which you would like to change. [This is a private piece of work which the pupil may choose to share with the teacher, or not.]

Multi-faith examples

Expressing beliefs: a mirror represents a soul which is pure, reflected truth, and the enlightened mind; as reflected light a mirror represents *Samsara*; a mind clouded with illusion is likened to a tarnished mirror which, once polished, will reflect truth.

Expressing beliefs: a spotless mirror depicts the idea of the Virgin Mary, who is also called the mirror of justice; Mary is also seen as the mirror of the church, meaning that aspects of her life have a meaning and implication for the church and individual Christians.

Expressing beliefs: a mirror is a reminder that the material world is a reflection of Brahman, like a reflection of the moon on water; seeing a reflection of something is to see its form, not its substance, and because form can be reflected, it is inherently illusory.

Expressing beliefs: everything with which a pious Muslim occupies themself in the material world is a mirror in which God is reflected, therefore they are always in contact with God. 'The universe is the mirror of God ... man is the mirror of the universe' (Ibn al-Nasafi).

Expressing beliefs: a mirror is a symbol for nature, which reflects the glory of God; traditionally, when a person dies, mirrors are covered in the house of mourning, perhaps because mirrors reflect life's possibilities, which are foreclosed in the face of death.

Expressing beliefs: using the analogy of a mirror the Guru Granth describes some of the attributes of God. 'He is always with you as your companion. Like the fragrance which remains in the flower, and like the reflection in the mirror' (684:976, 977). 'He sees everything as clearly as one's face reflected in a mirror' (1318:901).

Money

Suggested themes

Consumerism

Materialism

Ultimate values

(Un)selfishness

Wealth

Worth

Equipment

- A bowl which appears to contain a great deal of money (newspaper notes concealed under one or two real ones)
- A bowl which is empty but has a label saying 'Living a rich life is...'

What to do

→ Sit in a circle in a room where the lighting is soft.

→ Place the first bowl with money in the centre of the group, on a table where it is visible to everyone. Ask the group to look at it and to allow thoughts and associations to flow through their minds and to note their feelings and ideas. Ask pupils to imagine that the bowl of money had been won by them in a competition – what would they plan to do with the money?

→ After a few minutes, remove the first bowl and replace it with the second empty bowl. Tell pupils again to allow thoughts and associations to flow through their minds and to note their feelings and ideas. Ask them to think about how they would complete the label, 'Living a rich life is ...'.

→ After a few minutes, remove the bowl. Allow time for individuals to note down their ideas.

→ Let pupils share their responses in twos or threes, and then follow this up by a general discussion of the interpretations, feelings and questions which the symbol arouses.

Questions

- What did the first bowl of money represent to you? Try and say why.
- What association(s) did it bring to mind?
- What did the second empty bowl represent to you? Try and say why.
- What association(s) did it bring to mind?
- What ideas did you have about using the money?
- How did you complete the sentence 'A rich life is …'?

Follow-up work

Creativity

→ **Draw, paint or write a poem** to represent the concept of a 'rich life'.

→ **Compose a short story** (250 words maximum) called 'A day in the life of a £10 note'.

→ **Plan and present a dance or drama** creating the different moods which money, by its absence or presence, can generate.

Analysis and expression

→ Individually or in pairs, choose six TV advertisements. Identify the type of motivation each uses to encourage people to buy the product they advertise. What values are implicit in them? Decide whether they are compatible with one or more of the religions referred to below. Choose a way of expressing your thoughts and ideas to the class.

Multi-faith examples

Expressing aspects of belief and practice: the importance of Enlightenment gained by the 'Middle Path' (rather than by the life of self denial and pain, or a life of luxury); non-attachment; showing generosity (*dana*).

Expressing aspects of belief and practice: the importance of earning money honestly and using it wisely to the benefit of self and others; showing generosity; following Jesus' teaching given in parables such as 'The rich man', and his injunction to put God first.

Expressing aspects of belief and practice: one of the four legitimate aims of life (*dharma* – righteousness; *artha* – wealth; *kama* – pleasure and *moksha* – liberation); Lakshmi is worshipped for family wellbeing and prosperity; giving charity is giving to God (Gita 9:27).

Expressing aspects of belief and practice: wealth is given in trust by Allah and Allah's promise is that it will never be decreased by charity; wealth needs to be balanced by generosity; *Sadaqah* (charity) is related to the Arabic words for 'truthfulness' and 'belief'.

Expressing aspects of belief and practice: wealth is a positive thing which is to be enjoyed with gratitude as long as it is used in a responsible manner, and it is remembered that wealth is not a reflection of a person's inner worth.

Expressing aspects of belief and practice: wealth is provided by God but is transient; honest living and detachment from worldly things are required; fasting and over-indulging are to be avoided; life is an opportunity for spiritual development; charitable giving is encouraged.

Rock

Suggested themes

Foundations

God

Immortality

Permanence

Sacrifice

Stability

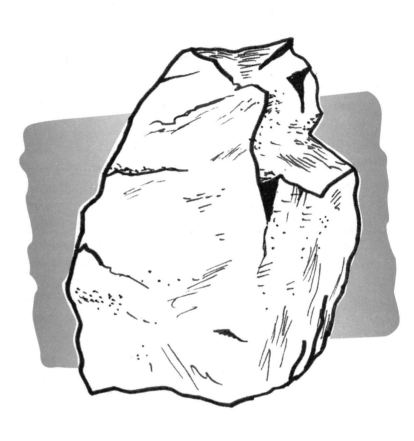

Equipment

- A large piece of interesting rock

What to do

→ Sit in a circle in a room where the lighting is soft.

→ Place the rock in the centre of the group, on a table where it is visible to everyone. Ask the group to look at it, to allow thoughts and associations to flow through their minds and to note their feelings and ideas.

→ After five minutes, remove the rock. Allow time for individuals to note down their ideas.

→ Share in twos or threes feelings and ideas. This should be followed by a general discussion of the interpretations and feelings which the rock aroused.

Questions

- What did the piece of rock represent to you? Try and say why.
- What association(s) did it bring to mind?
- What other kinds of rocks are there? What different things do they suggest to you?
- What special qualities do rocks have?
- What past or current events did the experience bring to mind?

Follow-up work

Reflection

→ **Draw, paint or write a poem** in response to the following: Imagine you are a large piece of rock or stone, chosen by a builder to be the foundation stone of a new religious building. Decide the details of this building (e.g. its size, shape, religious tradition, place) and how the stone might 'feel'. Choose a way of expressing your thoughts and ideas.

Investigation and evaluation

→ **Find out about** the Bamiyan Statues of the Buddha which were destroyed by the Taliban in March 2001, despite international protests. This website will set the scene: www.e-greenstar.com/Afghanistan/bamiyan.htm

→ **Do you think** the Bamiyan Buddhas should be rebuilt? Consider the arguments for and against, and express your conclusion in 200 words (maximum) suitable for an article in a Sunday broadsheet newspaper.

Multi-faith examples

Marking holy places and expressing beliefs: statues of the Buddha at Bamiyan, Afghanistan (destroyed in 2001, and to be rebuilt); stupas built to commemorate the Buddha's eight great deeds accomplished during his life, and to enshrine his relics after his death.

Marking holy places and expressing beliefs: God described as the Rock (Psalm 18:31); St Peter (Cephas – 'rock') as the earthly foundation of the church; the rock sealing Jesus' tomb, thrown aside at his resurrection; rock used as foundations of churches and altars.

Marking holy places and expressing beliefs: rocks as the foundations of temples and altars; rock and cave temples such as those at Mahabalipuram, expressing fundamental truths in their design and reliefs; the *shiva linga*, a conical rock symbolising Shiva as creator.

Marking holy places and expressing beliefs: surah 15 of the Qur'an, called *al-Hijr* (The Rock); the Black Stone (*Al-Hajr ul-aswad*) kissed by pilgrims when visiting the Ka'ba in Makkah on *Hajj*; casting stones into the cairn at Mina, on *Hajj*, to repulse temptation.

Marking holy places and expressing beliefs: God described as 'The Rock' in the TeNaKh (Deuteronomy 32:4); rock used as the foundation stone for the Temple of Jerusalem, and the remaining Western Wall; stones placed on a tomb on the anniversary of the person's death.

Marking holy places and expressing beliefs: the Sri Harmandir Sahib (Golden Temple) in Amritsar, has a door each side (east, west, north, south) representing its accessibility to all regardless of race, creed or class. Its architecture represents a harmony between the Muslim and Hindu ways of construction work.

Scales

Suggested themes

Decision-making

Equality

Good and Evil

Heaven and Hell

Justice

Last Judgement

Equipment

• A balance or scales

What to do

→ Sit in a circle in a room where the lighting is soft.

→ Place the scales, with each dish equally balanced, in the centre of the group, on a table where they are visible to everyone. Ask the group to look at them and to allow thoughts and associations to flow through their minds and to note their feelings and ideas.

→ After a few minutes, place some weights on one dish of the scales so that they are no longer equally balanced. Tell pupils again to allow thoughts and associations to flow through their minds and to note their feelings and ideas.

→ After a few minutes, remove the scales. Allow time for individuals to note down their ideas.

→ Let pupils share their responses in twos or threes, and then follow this up by a general discussion of the interpretations, feelings and questions which the symbol arouses.

Questions

- What did the scales represent to you? Try and say why.
- What association(s) did they bring to mind?
- What did they represent when equally balanced? Try and say why.
- What did they suggest when weighed down on one side?
- What kinds of things do we talk about as being 'balanced' or not?
- What kinds of values do we associate with balance in our lives?

Follow-up work

Creativity

→ **Draw, paint or write a poem** to represent the idea of balance in some aspect of life.

→ **Plan and present a dance or drama** about situations where justice is denied, and where it is given.

Investigation, application and reflection

→ In pairs, find out about one religious organisation which works to restore harmony or justice (see examples below) and express understanding visually, using the image of a balance or scales. Reflect on: 'How important is justice to the religion I have studied? What might I learn from this?'

Buddhism: www.amitabhahospice.org
Christianity: www.christianaid.org
Hinduism: www.foodrelief.org
Islam: www.muslimaid.org
Judaism: www.wiesenthal.com
Sikhism: www.panthkhalsa.org

Multi-faith examples

Expressing beliefs. Balance and inner harmony: reached when a person is in balance with the people and natural forces around them. *Nirvana* (Enlightenment): a state of peace and harmony, reached when greed, hatred and ignorance are extinguished.

Expressing beliefs. Balance, equality, justice and **harmony** are key concepts in Christianity, often represented by a weighing balance or scales. **Judgement:** Archangel Michael is often shown holding a pair of scales in which he weighs the souls of the departed for the afterlife.

Expressing beliefs. Dharma: the ultimate moral balance of all things. There is a divine order of the natural and cosmic realms, and within an individual's life. **Responsibility:** each person has the responsibility to balance his or her own *dharma*.

Expressing beliefs. Judgement: Allah sent messengers with signs, and with the Book and the Balance (Qur'an, Al-Hadeed 57:25). The Book contains revelations about what is right and wrong. The Balance refers to a person's ability to measure and calculate so that the path shown by the Book and explained by the Prophet can be followed.

Expressing beliefs. God: The justice and righteousness of God is the fundamental connection between religion and law in Judaism. 'A just balance and scales are the Lord's; all the weights of the bag are His work.' (TeNaKh, Proverbs 16:11).

Expressing beliefs. Balance: gives life meaning, purpose and tranquillity; it is obtained through God's grace. Without it life is useless. **Justice:** is one of the attributes of God (Adi Granth 723). Those who realise it within them become one with Him.

Tree

Suggested themes

Creation

Enlightenment

Environment

Humankind

Life

Paradise

Wisdom

Universe

Equipment

- Outside the classroom, using an actual tree, or inside viewing a tree through a window
- Image of a tree projected onto a screen (alternative)

What to do

→ Sit in a circle in a room where the lighting is soft.

→ When everyone is seated and can see the tree, ask the group to look at it and to allow thoughts and associations to flow through their minds and to note their feelings and ideas.

→ After a few minutes, ask pupils to close their eyes and to imagine that they are actually attempting to climb the tree, through its branches, to the top – create a story to lead them to the top, overcoming obstacles, broken branches etc.

→ Ask pupils to remember what they think, feel and see as they climb. Ask them to imagine what it feels like to be at the top, what they can see, hear and feel. What is it like to look out, look down and look up? Explain to them that it is their tree and that they may come down from it when they wish.

→ Let pupils share their responses in twos or threes, and then follow this up with a general discussion of the interpretations, feelings and questions which the symbol arouses.

Questions

- What did the tree represent to you? Try and say why.
- What association(s) did it bring to mind?
- What kinds of things did you think of as you were climbing up your tree?
- What did you see, hear and feel, when you were climbing and when you reached the top?
- When did you choose to come down and why?

Follow-up work

Creativity

→ **Draw, paint or write a poem** to represent personal experience and feelings, expressing what the symbol meant personally.

→ **Plan and present a dance or drama** creating the different moods which trees can reflect.

Reflection

→ **Create a personal development tree.** Take a large sheet of paper on which a tree with many spreading branches and leaves is drawn. On each leaf and branch write down words which describe things learned, felt, and experienced, from early childhood (represented by the base of the trunk). Leave space for further growth throughout life. Choose whether to share thoughts with the class, or to keep them private.

Multi-faith examples

Expressing beliefs: the Buddha sat under the bodhi (fig tree) for six years before he attained enlightenment; he preached his first sermon there and died there also; fig trees are identified with the Tree of Knowledge.

Expressing beliefs: the Tree of Life is described as standing in the centre of the Garden of Eden, uniting heaven and earth (Genesis); the Kingdom of God is described by Jesus as being like a mustard seed and a fig tree; the tree is occasionally used to describe humankind.

Expressing beliefs: the world is viewed as a cosmic fig tree which has roots in the underworld, a trunk in this world, branches reaching into the heavens, leaves which are the Vedas, flowers which are the object of the senses, and roots which give birth to action.

Expressing beliefs: the Tree of Blessing represents spiritual blessing and illumination, the light of Allah which shines on the earth; trees are represented as offering shade in Paradise; the environment in all its goodness is a gift from Allah, to be enjoyed and preserved.

Expressing beliefs: the Tree of Life gives knowledge of good and evil and the Dew of Light (by which the dead are resurrected) emanates from it; the environment in all its goodness is a gift from God, to be enjoyed and preserved (see festival of Tu B'shevat).

Embracing other faiths: people of different religions can all achieve salvation while following their own religion. Guru Arjan Dev said, 'There is a garden, in which so many plants have grown ... There is only one gardener who tends it ... They all bear fruit – none is without fruit.'

Water

Suggested themes

Baptism

Creation

Death

Healing

Life

Purification

Rebirth

Renewal

Equipment

- A transparent glass or plastic bowl containing water
- Background sound of rushing water or waves, in a storm and in calm weather (e.g. on cassette tape or CD)
- Sounds from an indoor water feature could be used to represent calm water

What to do

→ Sit in a circle in a room where the lighting is soft.

→ Place the bowl of water in the centre of the group, on a table where it is visible to everyone. Play the sounds selected.

→ Ask the group to look at the bowl of water, and to think about any experiences they have had to do with water. Ask them to think about what it would feel like to float on it, dive in it, let it flow through their hands or exist in it, and to note down their feelings and ideas.

→ After a few minutes, remove the bowl of water. Allow time for individuals to note down their ideas.

→ Let pupils share their responses in twos or threes, and then follow this up by a general discussion of the interpretations, feelings and questions which the symbol arouses.

Questions

- What did the bowl of water represent to you? Try and say why.
- What association(s) did it bring to mind?
- What did you think and feel it would be like to be in the water?
- What special properties do you think water has?
- What past or current events did it bring to mind?

Follow-up work

Creativity

→ **Write a poem** based on the cleansing and purifying qualities of water and on what is meant by purity.

→ **Prepare and present a dance or drama** creating the different moods which water can reflect.

→ **Create a festival** involving water. Choose its significance, design a ceremony, select an occasion when it can be shared and present the idea to an audience (e.g. collective worship).

Investigation and interpretation

→ Individually or in pairs, choose one of the main world religions from the course of study. Investigate and report on the place and symbolic meaning of water in the chosen religion.

Multi-faith examples

Showing respect: pouring water over the statue of the Buddha.
Making offerings: offerings are replaced by small bowls of water symbolising the offering (Tibet).

Symbolising purity, cleansing from sin, and the beginning of a new life in Christ: using water at baptism (infant and believers).
Symbolising God's blessing: dedications, exorcisms, burials, healing (e.g. Lourdes) and service (e.g. foot washing).

Expressing sacredness: believing that all water is sacred, especially rivers, and particularly the Ganges.
Symbolising purity: visiting holy places, usually located on the banks of rivers, and bathing in the waters.

Symbolising purity: washing before prayer *(wudu)*, in preparation for worshipping Allah.
Respecting the dead: washing the whole body in pure water *(ghusl)* – e.g. for the dead before burial.

Symbolising purity: the washing of hands before the Sabbath meal; immersing in 'living water' (e.g. the sea, a river, a spring or a *mikveh* (ritual bath)) after contact with a dead body or after menstruation.

Expressing commitment: using sweetened water *(amrit)* in the baptism ceremony. **Symbolising purity:** washing before prayer in the gurdwara; bathing before entering the Golden Temple at Amritsar, and in the water surrounding it.

Wheel

Suggested themes

Eternity

Holiness

Human existence

Immortality

Perfection

Power

Seasons

Time

Equipment

- A wheel – a simple wheel which can be suspended on a cord or piece of wire so that it can be made to spin
  Note: The effect is better if the wheel is not obviously from a particular machine or mode of transport. A hoop works well if suspended by thin string and encouraged to spin slowly.
- Background music (optional)

What to do

→ Sit in a circle in a room where the lighting is soft.

→ Suspend the wheel in the centre of the group where it is safe and visible to everyone. Ask the group to look at it and to allow their thoughts and associations to flow through their minds and to note their feelings and ideas.

→ After a few minutes, spin the wheel slowly. Tell the pupils again to allow thoughts and associations to flow through their minds and to note their feelings and ideas.

→ After a few minutes, remove the wheel. Allow time for individuals to note down their ideas.

→ Let pupils share their responses in twos or threes, and then follow this up by a general discussion of the interpretations, feelings and questions which the symbol arouses.

Questions

- What did the wheel first represent to you? Try and say why.
- What association(s) did it bring to mind?
- What did the spinning wheel represent to you? Try and say why.
- What association(s) did it bring to mind?
- Did you find the still or the spinning wheel more fascinating?

Follow-up work

Creativity

→ **Draw, paint or write a poem** to represent personal thoughts and feelings whilst observing either the still or the spinning wheel.

→ **Design a symbol** to represent one of the religious themes or concepts typically represented by the wheel or circle (e.g. eternity, unity, God).

→ **Design a mandala** to represent aspects of personal life and experience (ideas and a template can be found at www.cleo.net.uk/subject.cfm?subject=11).

Investigation and interpretation

→ Individually or in pairs, choose one of the main world religions from the course of study. Investigate and report on the place and symbolic meaning of the wheel or circle in the chosen religion.

Multi-faith examples

Expressing aspects of belief and practice: *mandala* (Sanskrit for circle, community, connection; a support for meditation); wheel of life (ceaseless worldly existence); wheel of *dharma* (propagation of Buddha's teaching); wheel of law (eight-spoked wheel, the eightfold path).

Expressing aspects of belief and practice: the circle represents eternity, holiness, God. A circular halo or nimbus is placed behind the head of religious figures in art to suggest saintliness. A circle with three rays symbolises the Trinity, sometimes circles or triangles are used. When intertwined they remind of the oneness of God.

Expressing aspects of belief and practice: the wheel is often stylised as the lotus, symbol of eternity, purity, prosperity, fertility and a symbol of Vishnu. A *tilak* (circular red dot) is a mark of auspiciousness worn on the forehead, at the point where the spiritual eye opens.

Expressing aspects of belief and practice: the circle is regarded as the perfect shape (it has no beginning and no end), representing infinity, eternity, unity, and Allah; a dome is a form of the circle, both a beautiful and a practical shape (amplifying sound, and encouraging air circulation).

Expressing aspects of belief and practice: a circle symbolises wholeness and completion; traditionally, a bride circles the groom seven times under the *chuppah*; a round *challah* is eaten on Rosh Hashanah; an egg, eaten in a house of mourning, symbolises the circle of life.

Expressing aspects of belief and practice: a circle is a symbol of strength and integrity, obedience, equality, oneness, universality and eternity; worn in the form of a *kara* (steel band) – one of the Five Ks, an outward sign of commitment and a constant reminder of God.

Using guided visualisation and guided story in RE

The technique

Guided visualisation: using imaginative techniques to encourage active engagement of the creative imagination in response to a stimulus (which may be of an object, or a role in a drama, for example).

Guided story: using imaginative techniques to make someone else's story more vivid.

Guided visualisation and guided story use a technique which:

- **enables** pupils to enter imaginatively into the thoughts, feelings and experiences of those in a story and explore their own responses to it;

- **involves** scripting a version of the story, usually told in the present tense, so that the listener takes an active role;

- **usually follows** a 'stilling' activity (see pages 6 and 7);

- **provides a choice** of follow-up activities, matched to the intended learning outcomes;

- **provides a stimulus** for the activities which follow, and is not an end in itself.

Stories from faith communities

Often called **sacred** or **faith** stories, these:
- may come from the sacred book(s) of the faith or be part of the tradition handed on in some other way;
- may come from or be about the founders or spiritual leaders of that faith;
- offer some insight of the faith into the meaning and purpose of life.

Stories from faith traditions often:
- **universalise.** They are stories about 'shared human experience', and address universal questions of meaning and purpose such as, 'What does it mean to be human?'
- **personalise.** They are stories about me – addressing my personal questions and experiences, addressing issues of 'personal search' and 'What does it mean to be me?'
- **re-present.** They are eternally re-enacted situations, emotions, dilemmas; they may be set in the past but they do not remain there. They offer 'windows' into the 'living belief system', and give their insights into the fundamental questions of what it means to be human and what it means to be me.

'Secular' stories

These do not come directly from within a faith tradition, but they express insights into human nature and address questions of meaning and purpose. As religion concerns itself with the whole of human life and experience, such stories provide a useful resource for RE.

Story is a key means by which humans have attempted to make sense of the world and of their experiences.

Many of these stories are useful in RE:
- Stories of and about the 'founders' and spiritual leaders of the faith(s);
- Stories told within religions to express their understanding of life and its purpose;
- Stories as a means of transmitting belief, faith and culture between generations;
- Stories underpinning festivals;
- Myth, legend, parable, history – all forms of religious story;
- Story as a means of expressing personal insight, feelings, beliefs and values;
- Stories about 'life' that relate to religious beliefs, practices, concepts and insights.

Resources

The internet is a vast and growing source of stories which can be used in the RE classroom. This page identifies some starting points. The internet makes available:

- **authentic** stories from a variety of faith and other traditions;
- **variety** of presentation, language and complexity;
- **sacred texts** in the original language and English;
- **graphics** to illustrate, inspire and enhance understanding;
- **audio** files to provide another voice for the classroom;
- **access** for pupils and teachers, at home and at school;
- **repetition** to support learning and for enjoyment.

The **overview** of types of story useful in RE (page 44) will provide stimulus to thinking and planning to develop your own guided stories.

The **internet resources** outlined on this page will provide a readily accessible (and free) source of suitable material.

Online sacred texts
- **Bible Gateway:** http://bible.gospelcom.net/bible?
- **Internet Sacred Text Archive:** www.sacred-texts.com

Story collections
- **Internet Storyboard:** www.sln.org.uk/storyboard
- **BBC Religion and Ethics:** www.bbc.co.uk/religion
- **The Big Myth:** http://mythicjourneys.org/bigmyth

Buddhism
- **Buddhanet**: www.buddhanet.net
- **Dharma the Cat**: www.dharmathecat.com

Christianity
- **Culham Institute** (RE curriculum materials): www.culham.info
- **RE Jesus:** http://rejesus.co.uk
- **RE Quest:** www.request.org.uk

Hinduism
- **HinduKids:** www.hindukids.org/grandpa
- **Biographies of Great Indians:** www.freeindia.org/biographies
- **Lord Swaminarayan:** www.swaminarayan.org

Islam
- **Bilal's Bedtime Stories:** www.al-islam.org/gallery/kids/books/bilal
- **Islam for Children:** www.jamaat.org/islam/Muhammad.html
- **Kid's Corner:** www.islamicity.com/KidsCorner

Judaism
- **Rabbi Amy Scheinerman:** http://scheinerman.net/judaism
- **Story of Purim:** http://holidays.net/purim/reaudio.htm

Sikhism
- **The Ten Gurus:** www.sgpc.net/gurus
- **Guru Nanak:** www.sikhs.org/guru1.htm

The best of all possible worlds ~ Perfect

RE focus

**'The best of
all possible worlds'**

Hope(s)

Ideals and idealism

Community

What to do

→ Start with a relaxation or stilling exercise (pages 6 and 7) and explain to pupils what they will be doing.

→ Lead the guided visualisation (page 47).

→ Debrief the activity (page 47).

→ Pupils complete a follow-up activity (page 47).

Equipment

• Music to play quietly as pupils complete their written work (optional). Suggestions include: 'Imagine' by John Lennon; 'River of Dreams' by Ladysmith Black Mambazo.

Introduction

This guided visualisation was originally developed as part of a unit of work on 'Holy Cities' for pupils living in an urban environment, and has since been used as a stimulus to work on a range of themes commonly found in RE syllabuses. There are natural links with Citizenship Education, too.

'Perfect' enables pupils to:

• **make links** between the idealism represented by religion and the realities of their own lives and communities;

• **realise** that the environment in which we live impacts on us as individuals;

• **consider** the importance of ideals, hopes and encouragement to the human spirit, and the need to believe that good things can be preserved and shared, and bad things changed.

A Perfect England
I imagine a perfect England
with love, kindness and peace
without war, hate and threats.

I imagine a perfect England
without bombs and guns
where children can play safely.

I imagine a perfect England
where police are not needed
where there is no crime
where old people are not afraid to come out
     of their homes.

I imagine a perfect England
where everyone has jobs
where no one lives on the streets

I imagine a perfect England
where there are no rulers or MPs
everyone gets on in harmony

I imagine, I imagine,
but will it ever come true?
Nicholas, Year 10
*[Note: Nicholas wrote this poem as his response to RE
work on the 'perfect' city. He is a blind pupil.]*

Narrative

Imagine that it is the end of the school day ... you're getting ready to go ... today you're going to walk home on your own ... you know your way ... nothing unusual ... just picture yourself getting out of school on your own at the end of the day ... it's quite easy ... the day ends ... just like any other day ... you leave the school ... and walk off without looking back ...
(Pause)

You notice ... litter round the school gate has all blown away ... or been cleared ... rubbish on the grass or pavement ... old cans ... tyres ... bags ... paper ... is all gone ... instead there are flowers you never noticed before ... Everything seems pretty normal ... but then you feel something unusual ... as if the sun is a bit brighter than usual ... the breeze softer ... you look around ... but you can't quite see what's different ...

You walk on ... there is definitely something different ... every little thing seems fresher ... brighter ... better than usual ... your shoe is suddenly comfy ...

You stop because you see a rare sight ... a rabbit on the grassy land you're passing ... it sits there ... unafraid ... nibbling grass ... you watch for a moment or two ... and you notice more rabbits in the grass ... or the hedge ... they're not scared ... they don't run off ...
(Pause)

You go on walking home ... and your heart is rather full of happiness ... because in some strange way the walk seems different today ... the whole place seems cleaned up ... better ... there's no sign of any vandalism ... no one fighting ... no name-calling from the other children ... no fighting.

You see an old lady sitting ... with a small boy ... they are talking together ... you realise that your part of town has been changed ... made perfect ... and as you get closer to home ... you feel excited ... will home be different too? ... Now imagine that you're walking towards your home ... it looks good ... you can see the door ... you feel as if you can imagine what might be different when you get there ... just spend some time imagining what it would be like to get home ... and to find that everything has been made new ... made perfect.
(Pause)

In a minute we're going to stop this imaginary story ... I wonder what the best thing you imagined was ... think about that for a moment ... and decide on one thing from your imagination that would be there ... or would be different ... in your perfect home.
(Pause)

When you've chosen ... then I'd like you to get ready for the end of this activity ... remember what the class room was like before you closed your eyes ... remember the furniture and the walls ... the people ... the décor... picture it all in your mind's eye ... then ... when you're ready ... look up [open your eyes] ... stretch if you want to ... Still ... be calm.
(Pause)

Follow-up activities

→ **The New Birmingham** (or wherever you live). Pupils express their ideas for their 'perfect town or city'. This could be a poem, artwork, a piece of music (composed or selected), or a multimedia sequence of images and captions.

→ In pairs, pupils consider 'What would God's message to our city be?' They compose the text of a 60-second statement (in text, audio or video format).

Questions

Use questions like these to focus follow-up discussion:

• How did you feel as you left school? Did your feelings change as you walked towards home?

• What would a perfect city be like?

• What would make our city or town more perfect? Who has responsibility here?

• What would God's message to our city or town be?

The value of human life – Being me

RE focus

Belonging

Identity

Sanctity of life

What to do

→ Start with a relaxation or stilling exercise (pages 6 and 7) and explain to pupils what they will be doing.

→ Lead the guided visualisation (page 49).

→ Pupils complete a follow up activity (page 49).

→ Debrief the activity (page 49).

Equipment

• Music to play quietly as pupils complete their work (optional).

• Resources for written work (paper, coloured pens etc.)

Introduction

This **guided visualisation** is an effective way of introducing pupils to a range of concepts including belonging, identity and the sanctity of life. It also provides stimulus for exploring what sacred texts and faith communities have to say about the concept(s) chosen, and opportunities for pupils to make links with their own ideas and experience.

When the pupils have finished their follow-up activity, this is a suitable point for the teacher to introduce the ideas of 'sacred', 'special' and 'holy', explaining that for many religious believers life has great, or even ultimate value. The images and words the pupils have produced can be used to explore the concept of the sanctity of life.

Who am I?
Who am I? They often tell me
I'm a friendly confident person
Most times happy but sometimes sad
Like a happy bird in flight
Who am I? They often tell me
A happy child
A good friend as well
Loyal to family and friends
Who am I? They also tell me
Sometimes I'm not as happy
As I normally am
Like a person that has two lives in one
Am I then really all that which other men tell of?
Or am I only what I myself know of myself?
I'm an energetic person
Love swimming a lot
I don't let out my strongest feelings
Only little ones
Sometimes I'm happy
Sometimes I'm sad
but happy is most often
never really sad
Who am I? This or the other?
Am I one person today, and tomorrow another?
Am I both at once?
I feel I'm two people
One sad, one happy
but whatever I am I know somebody loves me
Who am I?
Whoever I am, thou knowest, O God, I am thine.
Sorrel, Year 7

Script

I want you to imagine that you can look down upon your own body ... seated here in this room ... as if you were looking down from a high balcony ... just picture yourself ... sitting in quiet, calm concentration here ... notice in your mind's eye how you look ... what attitude you have ...

(Pause)

Now think about the person you are today ... think of all that has made you who you are ... your family ... your home ... those who love you ... your friends ... your pets ... the places where you've lived ... just notice all the things that make you a unique individual ... someone special ... someone that no one else is quite like ... let yourself notice these things ... and take a little time to remember them ...

(Pause)

One life ... you didn't ask for it ... you were given it ... who do you think gave it to you? ... parents? ... God? ... or nature? ... you didn't pay for it, ... but it's priceless ... the most valuable gift you have ... spend a little time looking at your life ... where it came from ... and where it's got to so far ...

(Pause)

Then come right back down ... in your imagination ... to your own body ... back to the here and now ... back to the school ... the classroom ... the chair ... remember the wall displays and the other people ... picture some of the details and then ... when you are ready ... look up ... [open your eyes] ... stretch if you want to ... Still ... be calm.

(Pause)

Follow-up activities

→ Pupils work individually to express their thoughts and ideas in the light of their imaginative thinking. They might use words or images or both.

Allow around 20 minutes for quiet work, which pupils can share with the group, if they are willing. Music playing quietly in the background may help concentration. Invite pupils to share their work, either in small groups or as a full class. This should be optional.

Questions

Use questions like these to focus follow-up discussion:

• What worked for you in this story? What stopped your imagination from working?

• What did you think about?

• What was too rushed? What was too slow?

• What words and pictures have you produced? What can we all share?

Personal growth – My secret garden

RE focus

Personal growth

Change

Purpose in life

What to do

→ Start with a relaxation or stilling exercise (pages 6 and 7) and explain to pupils what they will be doing.

→ Lead the guided visualisation (page 51).

→ Pupils complete a follow-up activity (page 51).

→ Debrief the activity (page 51).

Equipment

• Large sheets of paper, writing equipment and coloured pens (available on pupils' table before the main activity).

• Music to play quietly as pupils complete their work (optional).

Note

Some pupils do not like the idea of a wall; this part of the guided visualisation can be omitted.

Introduction

This **guided visualisation** draws upon an image that is a fruitful one for exploring ideas of personal growth – a garden. Other exercises where pupils focus on a specific image of a tree or a flower can be used in a similar way. For example:

• **Flowers** (pages 24–25)

• **Fruit** (pages 26–27)

• **Trees** (pages 38–39)

Links can be made with parables of growth and children encouraged to find connections in these parables that speak to their own experiences. For example:

• **Parable of the sower** (Mark 4:1–20)

• **Parable of the mustard seed** (Matthew 13:31–32)

• **Parable of the seed growing secretly** (Mark 4:26–29)

> *Sometimes when I am in a beautiful place, like when I go for walks on the hills near my home, I feel deeply moved, that the beauty and goodness of everything has a meaning. It sounds very slushy, but it is difficult to describe. I get a similar feeling and purpose when I see very good films or read good poetry, especially that of Wilfred Owen. I feel there is a purpose to life and that I have to do something for the world, especially that there is something outside me that is an active force. At the same time I am always filled with hope. It leaves me very happy.'*

> *I've looked into the evening sky and seen the stars and as my eyes become accustomed to the dark, more stars appear. I realise that they are so far away that man is unlikely to see these other worlds that are very similar and also very unlike our own system. This gives me a feeling of insecurity and one of pointless existence, but also I experience something which tells me I have got to make the most of my life with what I've got within me and around me. It doesn't last long but it's good while it lasts.*

These two examples of young people's writing are taken from *Religion and Values at 16+*, Edward Robinson & Mike Jackson, CEM, 1987

Script

You are walking down a path which leads to a wall ... stand in front of the wall and look at it for a few moments ... try touching it ... it is solid and strong ... behind this wall is a secret garden which is waiting for you to explore it. This garden is yours.

(Pause)

As you look at the wall more closely you see a door ... what does the door look like? ... find a way to open it ... perhaps you have to say some words ... perhaps the door opens by itself ... go through the door and into the garden ... stand and look around you ... to left and right...

(Pause)

What do you see? ... are there paths to follow? ... is it wild or well cared for? ... choose where you want to start exploring ... take some time to explore ... are there any hidden areas? ... woodland? ... watery boggy bits? ...

(Pause)

What types of plants grow in your garden? ... do you see seedlings? ... mature plants? ... trees? ... shrubs? ... vegetables? ... flowers? ,,, herbs? ... fruit?

(Pause)

Every good garden has a compost heap ... where is yours? ... how big is it? ... are there any plants that you would like to take out and put on the compost heap? ... are there some new plants that you would like to put in the soil? ... does the soil need anything? ... are there any dry places or undernourished areas?

(Pause)

Now stand back and take a long look at the garden ... are there any changes you would like to make?

Remember ... any plants you pull up and put on the compost heap will in turn help new plants to grow ... perhaps you would like to create more space in the garden or put in more plants? ... decide what you would like to do ... remember too that some changes will take a long time to show...

(Pause)

This garden is yours to visit whenever you wish ... say goodbye to the garden and go to the door in the wall ... is there any message you would like to give your garden ... or action you would like to take? ...

do so and then turn and open the door and leave the garden ... and come back to this room ... and when you are ready, look up [open your eyes] ... stretch if you want to ... Still ... be calm.

(Pause)

Follow-up activities

→ Pupils draw, write or model something that represents their feelings about their garden. This could be text (a poem or short account), a collage or drawing, a model, diagram or song lyrics.

→ Pupils should work individually, in silence or quietly talking with those near by. It is helpful to have music playing quietly in the background.

→ Pupils talk about their work with a partner, sharing as much or as little as they wish.

Questions

Use questions like these to focus follow-up discussion:

- Who found the exercise worked for them? Who didn't?

- How did you feel as you entered the garden? Did your feelings change as you walked around? How?

- What changes did you decide to make?

- Who is the gardener?

- What connection does your experience of the garden have with your life at present?

Finding inner strength – Visit to a wise person

RE focus

Inner resources

Ultimate questions

Spiritual development

What to do

→ Start with a relaxation or stilling exercise (pages 6 and 7) and explain to pupils what they will be doing.

→ Lead the guided visualisation (page 53).

→ Debrief the activity (page 53).

→ Pupils complete a follow-up activity (page 53).

Equipment

- Resources for written work (paper, coloured pens etc.)
- Music to play quietly as pupils complete their work (optional).

Introduction

This **guided visualisation** is a version of one found in various resources, some now out of print. 'Visit to a wise person' provides an opportunity for spiritual development; an awareness that we all have inner resources of which we are all too often unaware, and which can be drawn upon in a range of situations and times of life.

It can also provide an engaging way into work on ultimate questions. The questions which pupils choose to ask the wise person can be quite pragmatic (e.g. Who are you?) but with older pupils are frequently more profound, as the five young people quoted below demonstrate.

Will there ever be peace on earth?
Male, Sikh, aged 13

How could we make the world a better place, with no poverty?
Male, Hindu, aged 13

Why bother creating life when most often it causes trouble?
Male, Muslim, aged 13

How did the world and universe begin, and what is the point of life?
Female, Buddhist, aged 13

What did Jesus look like?
Female, Christian, aged 12

Script

I want you to imagine that you are walking along a mountain path ... it is a beautiful clear night ... the moon is shining brightly ... you can see the path ahead quite clearly ... look around you as you walk ... what do you see? ... what do you hear? ... what can you smell? ... how do you feel? ...

(Pause)

Ahead of you ... leading from the main path ... is a small side path that leads up higher to a cave ... the home of a very wise person ... so wise that they can tell you the answer to any question ... turn off and walk slowly along this side path ... towards the wise person's cave...

When you arrive at the cave ... there is a small fire just in front ... you might just be able to see someone sitting in the firelight ... walk towards the fire ... put some more wood on it ... sit quietly opposite the fire ... as the fire burns more brightly you can see the wise person more clearly ... look closely ... notice the details of their appearance ... their face ... eyes ... body ... clothes...

(Pause)

Ask the wise person a question that is important to you ... as you ask your question, watch the wise person's face ... what reaction is given? ... is the answer given in words? ... with a gesture? ... or are you shown something? ... what kind of answer are you given? ...

(Pause)

Sit quietly for a moment ... think about the answer to your question ... do you understand what has been said? ... are there other questions you want to ask? ... how do you feel towards the wise person? ...

It is now time to leave ... say anything else you want to say ... see the wise person reaching into an old bag ... they take out a special gift and give it to you to keep . ... look closely at the gift ... hold it carefully ... how do you feel about the wise person now? ... it's time to go ... leave the cave and walk slowly down the mountain path ... look at it carefully to remember your way back when you want to visit again...

(Pause)

Keep the gift with you as you return to the classroom ... examine it carefully ... thoughtfully ... what is it? ... touch it ... smell it ... turn it over in your hands ... and then ... when you are ready ... look up [open your eyes] ... stretch if you want to ... Still ... be calm.

(Pause)

Follow-up activities

→ Pupils draw, write or model something that represents their experience. This could be text (a poem or short account), a collage or drawing, a model, diagram or song lyrics.

→ Pupils should work individually, in silence or quietly talking with those near by. It is helpful to have music playing quietly in the background.

→ Pupils talk about their work with a partner, sharing as much or as little as they wish.

Questions

Use questions like these to focus follow-up discussion:

- Who found the exercise worked for them? Who didn't?

- What was too rushed? What was too slow?

- Was the wise person male or female?

- What question did you ask the wise person?

- How did you feel about the answer you received?

- What gift did the wise person give you?

- How did you feel about the gift?

Sacred texts – The last piece of paper in the world

RE focus

Sacred texts

Scripture(s)

What to do

→ Start with a relaxation or stilling exercise (pages 6 and 7) and explain to pupils what they will be doing.

→ Lead the guided visualisation (page 55).

→ Pupils complete the follow-up activity (page 55).

→ Debrief the activity (page 55).

Equipment

• Paper and writing equipment (available on pupils' table before the main activity).

• Music to play quietly as pupils complete their written work (optional).

Introduction

This **guided visualisation** provides an introduction to understanding the place and importance of sacred texts in religious traditions. It is particularly suitable for upper primary or lower secondary pupils; the two examples of pupils' work included here were completed by lower secondary pupils.

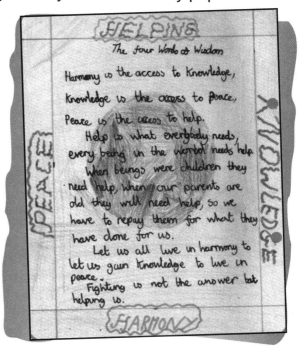

RE skills which might develop through this activity

Empathy
• How would the person writing on the first ever piece of paper feel?
• What might she want to write?

Reflection
• What words are most important in life?
• What do I want to pass on to people who come in following generations?

Expression
• How can I express the most important things of all?
• How can I show how important this message is?
• What words, pictures, and symbols could I use?
• Are words enough?

Interpretation
• What is meant by 'sacred words'?
• Why are holy books passed on; why do they inspire respect?
• Do I understand what the words of scripture mean to believers?

Script

Once, long ago, in the desert land of Egypt, someone made the first ever piece of paper in the world.

Imagine the inventor ... gathering papyrus reeds ... beating and drying them ... and then looking at the paper...

What would she write on it? ... What message could she set down for all the people who would come after her? ...

No one knows just where the first piece of paper was made, or what was written on it.

(Pause)

Now just imagine that something happened, so that there was no more paper ... something which meant that we couldn't find, or make, any more...

Imagine all the world environment was so polluted that reeds, and wood pulp and trees were no more ... and paper was impossible to make ever again...

Just think how different life would be.

(Pause)

And now imagine that the very last piece of plain paper is yours ... to write on it whatever you want to...

Picture yourself sitting quietly in front of a blank piece of paper ... knowing it is the last sheet of blank paper in the world ... and it is precious.

(Pause)

And imagine that you have the chance to write on this last piece of paper ... the most important message that there is ... the words you really want to pass on to future generations of humans ... that you would not want to be forgotten...

The last piece of paper would be special, almost holy .... and the words you write on it will be special too....

What would you write?

(Pause)

When you are ready, take a piece of paper and write on it the words you would write.

Follow-up activity

→ Immediately the main activity is ended, pupils use the materials already on their table and write their words for 'the last piece of paper in the world'. This could be done in silence.

Questions

Use questions like these to focus follow-up discussion:

- What worked for you in this activity? What stopped your imagination from working?
- What did you imagine happened to cause there to be no more paper?
- How did you feel as you sat in front of the blank piece of paper?
- What words did you write? Was the choice easy or difficult? Why?

Poetry – Life's like ....

RE focus

Metaphor

What to do

→ Start with a relaxation or stilling exercise (see pages 6 and 7) and explain to pupils what they will be doing.

→ Lead the guided visualisation (see page 57).

→ Pupils complete the follow-up activity (see page 57).

→ Debrief the activity.

Equipment

- A copy of the stimulus poem visible to all.
- A copy of the examples given on the right (optional).

Introduction

This simple **visualisation** can be very powerful and provide pupils with the opportunity in a supportive environment to share fears and anxieties at a stressful time of their school life, and also to affirm the values which they have come to espouse.

What others have said

Life's like ...

...**a minestrone.** *(10CC)*

...**a tragedy** in close-up, but **a comedy** from a distance. *(Charlie Chaplin)*

...**a tin of sardines** – we're all looking for the key. *(Alan Bennett)*

...**a sewer**: what you get out depends on what you put in. *(Anon)*

...**a disease**, and death the only cure. *(Albert Camus)*

...**a rat race** – and if you win, it shows you're the top rat. *(Anon)*

...**being a tree** – get your roots down, and branch out. Growing is natural. *(GK Chesterton)*

...**a journey** with no map, no signpost and no destination. *(Anon)*

...**Sanskrit** read to a pony. *(Lou Reed)*

...**a gift**: you ought to say thank you, and you've got it for free. *(Anon)*

Script

Now that you are relaxed ... I want you to listen very carefully to the words of a poem written by a 16-year-old school pupil ... it is their reflection on what life is all about ... you may agree ... you may see life very differently ... listen ...

(Pause)

Life's like...
80 minutes in an exam room
Doing GCSE RE.
It's like life, really:
80 years in life's big hall
Trying to pass a test of life.

I feel unprepared
Other people seem more confident
Teachers raise their voices
Instructions are given.

I'm not sure I understand
I wish I was somewhere else
Questions come up
I try to answer
I wish I knew more
I wish I could say what I really mean.

I do my best
It isn't very good
I stare blankly into space
Other people ask for more paper
Time passes

Lifetime passes
At the end we are all told
'You can go now'
A funeral is arranged
Beyond all this, an envelope
Did I pass? What grade?
I open the envelope.
Is it paradise for me? Or hell?

The card inside says three words:
Grace. Love. Welcome.
(Pause)

What questions or comments do you have for the poet? ... what metaphor for life would you choose for yourself? ... when you've chosen ... then I'd like you to get ready for the end of this activity ... remember what the classroom was like before you closed your eyes ... remember the furniture and the walls ... the people ... the décor ... picture it all in your mind's eye ... then ... when you're ready ... look up [open your eyes] ... stretch if you want to ... Still ... be calm.

Follow-up activity

→ Pupils work individually to express their thoughts and ideas in the light of their imaginative thinking. They might write a poem, draw a picture, choose a series of images to which they add commentary, choose or compose a piece of music.

It is helpful if pupils work in silence or talk quietly with those near by. It can be helpful to have music playing quietly in the background.

Pupils talk about their work with a partner, sharing as much or as little as they wish.

Questions

Use questions like these to focus follow-up discussion:

- What associations did the metaphor of the exam room bring to mind?
- How closely did you identify with the ideas the poet was expressing? What would you want to say to them or ask them?
- What metaphor best describes your own ideas about what life is all about?

Judgement and promise – Noah

RE focus

Promise

Judgement

What to do

→ Start with a relaxation or stilling exercise (pages 6 and 7) and explain to pupils what they will be doing.

→ Lead the guided story (page 59).

→ Debrief the activity (page 59).

→ Pupils complete a follow-up activity (page 59).

Equipment

• Resources for written work (paper, coloured pens etc.).

• Music to play quietly as pupils complete their work (optional).

Introduction

This **guided story** invites pupils to enter imaginatively into the thoughts, feelings and experiences of a character in the story as a way of supporting their learning about the concepts at the heart of the account. This is particularly suitable for upper primary or lower secondary pupils.

The story is told in the scriptures of three religions:

Judaism: Genesis chapter 7 (Tenakh)

Christianity: Genesis chapter 7 (Bible)

Islam: Surah 71, Nuh (Qur'an)

This guided story uses the biblical text. Older pupils might compare the accounts given in the sacred texts of the three religions, identifying similarities and differences and suggesting reasons for what they notice.

The BBC's *Testament* series is a further resource. Teachers will need to be aware of how this film presentation differs from the biblical text. Older pupils could compare these two 'tellings' of the story, and account for differences.

Script

In your imagination, I want you to picture a time long ago ... and far away ... a land which is rich and fertile ... imagine you are out in the open air ... working with your father ... Noah ... he's busy on a new project ... building an Ark ... he has been busy for weeks ... listen to him hammering ... look at him carefully as he works ... what thoughts do you have? ... about the Ark? ... about your father? ... about God?

(Pause)

Time passes ... a few days ... look at your father now ... he is smiling ... the Ark is finished ... walk over and join him ... look at the Ark together ... how does it look to you? ... so much hard work ... so little time ... how do you feel? ... excited? ...nervous? ... frightened? ...

(Pause)

As you stand with your father ... you see your brother in the distance ... he's herding the animals towards the Ark ... so many ... what can you see? ... what can you hear? ... what can you smell? ... what do you think? ...

It's time to set sail ... the ark is full ... the animals ... your family ... all are safely on board ... it's getting darker and darker ... the temperature is dropping and you feel colder ... rain is starting to fall ... listen to it drumming on the roof ... louder and louder... what are your thoughts? ...

(Pause)

Time passes ... a few days ... the rain stops ... walk over to the window and join the others looking out ... what are they looking for? ... suddenly in the distance you see movement ... a bird flying towards you ... it has a twig in its beak ... the bird Noah sent to look for dry land ... go to tell him ... what does he say? ... how do you feel? ...

Suddenly there is a bump ... the Ark touches dry land ... gradually the waters recede ... everything becomes normal once more ... you see the mountains ... the trees ... the fields ... the rivers...

(Pause)

Look up into the sky ... what do you see? ... a rainbow? ... suddenly you remember ... before the rain started ... before you got into the Ark ... Noah told you that God had made a special promise ... what is this promise? ... what thoughts do you have? ... about your father? ... about God?

(Pause)

Now I want you to leave your imaginary story ... remember the classroom ... the chairs and tables ... the wall displays and the other people ... picture some of the details and then ... when you are ready ... look up [open your eyes] ... stretch if you want to ... Still ... be calm.

(Pause)

Follow-up activities

➔ Pupils express their ideas about an aspect of the story that particularly struck them. This could be a poem, a character profile or a dialogue. Work can be shared with the class, and the meaning of the story clarified.

➔ Pupils discuss and compare the biblical narrative with the imaginative script. What do they notice? What fits? What doesn't fit? What insight into the biblical story does the imaginative work provide?

➔ Pupils write alternative interpretations from the point of view of:
- a sceptic;
- an atheist.

Questions

Use questions like these to focus follow-up discussion:

- During the guided story, what were your feelings about Noah? Did they change at all? Why?

- How would you express the heart of this story in one sentence?

- What is your view of the story of the Flood in Genesis 7? What do stories like this mean?

Encountering the divine – Journey to Emmaus

RE focus

Religious experience

What to do

→ Start with a relaxation or stilling exercise (see pages 6 and 7) and explain to pupils what they will be doing.
→ Lead the guided story (page 61).
→ Debrief the activity (page 61).
→ Pupils complete a follow-up activity (page 61).

Equipment

• Copies of the biblical account of the Journey to Emmaus from Luke 24 (optional). *Note: Some pupils will not associate the imaginative script with the resurrection unless the teacher decides to use the biblical material first. Teachers might begin with Luke 24 or with the guided imagery, depending on their aims.*

Introduction

Based on the biblical account of Jesus' resurrection appearance to two people on the road to Emmaus, this **guided story** aims to enable pupils to understand that life-changing encounters with the divine are, for many believers, closer to the heart of faith than arguments. They can happen to anyone, and they happen repeatedly through the centuries. They are a constant feature of human experience.

Encounters with God

Other examples of the human encounter with the transcendent in the Bible, or in another religious context, can be used to develop in a similar way to the 'Journey to Emmaus'.

The following biblical examples will provide a starting point for further work:

• **Jacob's dream** of the angelic ladder, and his wrestling with God (Genesis 28 and 32);
• **The call of Moses** at the burning bush (Exodus 3);
• **One of Ezekiel's visions,** for example the 'valley of dry bones' (Ezekiel 37);
• **Isaiah's vision** of the throne of God (Isaiah 6);
• **The transfiguration** of Jesus (Mark 9);
• **The conversion** of the apostle Paul (Acts 9).

Script

I want you to imagine you can see a dusty road ... in a fading evening light ... in a hot country ... there are olive trees and palms around the landscape ... as you watch ... in the distance ... you see two people ... a man and a woman ... walking along the road together.

They are too far away for you to hear them ... and they don't notice you ... but they seem to be depressed ... in their walk ... their manner ... their appearance ... their feet drag ... they shake their heads as they talk to each other ... their baggage seems heavy ... Watch them as they walk ... for a while...

(Pause)

Then you notice a third person ... behind ... wearing loose clothing ... with a hood up over his head ... walking faster ... catching up ... he joins the depressed pair ... he falls in step with them ... the three travel on together ... and talk...

The new arrival is the opposite of the other two ... he seems energetic ... lively ... he is now deep in conversation with the couple ... he moves his hands keenly to illustrate some point ... he throws an arm round the shoulders of one of his companions ... as you watch them walk along ... all three gradually seem to relax together ... they seem to quicken their pace a little ... their baggage seems lighter ... there are smiles ... quiet laughter ... Watch them ... for a minute...

(Pause)

The three walk on into a small village ... there are clay brick houses lit by low lights in the dusky evening ... the couple pause at the gate of one house ... the third person seems to be going on ... but they stop him ... they're inviting him in ... he accepts ... and the three turn together to the door ... open it up ... and slip inside the house...

The door closes ... you watch for a moment ... the lights come on at the windows ... you see the figures inside sitting down at the table ... What do you imagine they are saying to each other?

(Pause)

Now I want you to leave your imaginary journey ... leave the three travellers in the evening light ... remember the classroom ... the chairs and tables ... the wall displays and the other people ... picture some of the details and then ... when you are ready ... look up [open your eyes] ... stretch if you want to ... Still ... be calm.

(Pause)

Follow-up activities

→ Pupils express their ideas about the people in the story, focusing on their experiences, feelings and beliefs. This could be a poem, a character profile or a dialogue.

→ Pupils discuss and compare the gospel narrative with the imaginative script. What do they notice? What fits? What doesn't fit? What insight into the biblical story does the imaginative work provide?

→ Pupils devise a script to continue the imaginative observation of the first Easter, set in the upper room, dealing with what happens in the later part of Luke 24.

Questions

Use questions like these to focus follow-up discussion:

• What worked for you in this story? What stopped your imagination from working?

• During the guided story, what did you imagine the people were thinking and talking about?

• When you read Luke 24, did it help to make sense of the guided story?

• Have you had the experience of someone talking to you in ways that changed your feelings from bad to good, despair to hope?

• What is your view of the resurrection story in Luke 24? What do stories like this mean? Can God speak to, or appear to, people like this?

Beliefs in action – Learning from Islam

RE focus

Beliefs in action

Being a good neighbour

What to do

→ Start with a relaxation or stilling exercise (pages 6 and 7) and explain to pupils what they will be doing.

→ Lead the guided story (page 63).

→ Pupils complete the follow-up activity (page 63).

→ Debrief the activity (page 63).

Equipment

- A copy of the original story, adapted by Abida Husseini (see page 64).
- The *adhan* (call to prayer), available on CD-ROM and the internet (optional).

Introduction

Based on a re-telling of a traditional Muslim story, this guided story asks pupils to engage with text from a faith community so that they can identify the key teachings which the story presents and consider what this means in practice. The follow-up activities require pupils to read for meaning, and so complement literacy work.

RE skills which might develop through this activity

Empathy
- How would the two main characters feel?
- What might they have prayed about as they entered the mosque together?

Reflection
- What principles do I value most?
- What principles do I want to pass on to people who come in following generations?

Expression
- How can I express the principles I base my life on?
- How can I show how important these are to me?
- What words, pictures, sounds and symbols could I use?

Interpretation
- What is meant by 'wisdom'?
- Why are religious stories passed on, and they remain popular down the generations?
- Do I understand the importance of religious stories for Muslims?

Script

I want you to imagine a time long ago ... in a far-off country ... a village called Jilan ... it's hot ... dusty ... bustling ... you live there ... with your family ... you know all the streets ... the houses ... the people ... the news ... the gossip...

(Pause)

As you watch ... you see a man you recognise ... everyone is talking about him ... his neighbour keeps playing loud music every time he tries to pray ... what will he do? ... he looks worried ... he walks up and down the street knocking on the doors ... he speaks to the householder ... they all shake their heads ... he walks away ... looking dejected ... then, you hear the muezzin call the Muslims of the village to prayer ... the man returns home ... to pray...

(Pause)

Time passes ... the man returns to the street ... he tries another door ... this time the householder looks animated ... they talk ... the man strides away ... hurriedly ... purposefully ... head held high ... without looking back ...

(Pause)

Time passes ... an hour or so ... you see two men in the street ... the man with his neighbour ... they are deep in conversation ... you can't quite hear everything they say, but you hear the words ... 'I'm sorry' ... 'so ashamed' ... 'thank you' ... 'why?' ... you are not clear who is speaking ... it doesn't seem to matter to them...

(Pause)

* Time passes ... several days ... you hear the call to prayer once again summoning Muslims to prayer ... you see the man and his neighbour walking together into the mosque to pray...

(Pause)

Now I want you to leave your imaginary journey ... leave the two men at prayer ... remember the classroom ... the chairs and tables ... the wall displays and the other people ... picture some of the details and then ... when you are ready ... look up ... stretch if you want to ... Still ... be calm.

(Pause)

Follow-up activities

→ Pupils work in twos to:
- discuss with a partner what they think the story is about;
- compare their ideas with the actual story (see page 64) and clarify their understanding of what the story is teaching;
- compose a sequel to the story – e.g. 'One month later...'

→ Pupils write alternative endings (from *) from the point of view of:
- a sceptic;
- an atheist.

→ Pupils choose the wisest piece of writing they have ever read, and identify three reasons why they chose it.

Questions

Use questions like these to focus follow-up discussion:

- Who found the exercise worked for them? Who didn't?
- What was too rushed? What was too slow?
- Did anything in the story surprise you? Why was that?
- How would you express the heart of this story in one sentence?

Sheikh Abdul Qadir

There was once a very patient and kind man who lived in Jilan, called Sheikh Abdul Qadir. He needed to be patient because his next-door neighbour was a non-believer who loved to play practical jokes. Whenever the sheikh said his prayers his neighbour would play music to disturb him. This would have made other people angry but the sheikh never complained.

One day the non-believing neighbour was arrested by the police in Jilan and thrown in jail. Of course, with the neighbour in jail no one disturbed the sheikh when he was praying, so he was able to pray in peace. The sheikh was relieved that no one was disturbing him, but then he started thinking that he had not seen the neighbour for several days. He started wondering. Where is he? Has he gone away on a journey? Is he ill?

Sheikh Abdul Qadir decided to find out what the matter was. He asked his other neighbours and when he heard what they said, he was very shocked. 'Your neighbour is in jail.' He asked, 'Why? What was his offence?' Nobody knew.

The sheikh was angry with himself that his neighbour had been in jail for several days and he hadn't done anything to help him. The sheikh went to the judge and told him that he would pay money to bail his neighbour out of jail. The Judge checked the details and found that the neighbour had been put in jail with no charges against him, so he was immediately freed.

The neighbour had been terrified when he was thrown into jail for no reason. He found out that it was only because of the sheikh that he had been released. He was ashamed of himself and went to the sheikh to apologise for being so unkind to him before. And when the unbeliever realised that Islam brought out such goodness in people and taught people how to look after others he became a Muslim.

Adapted by Abida Husseini

> *Well ... I think life is a lot like milk. You shouldn't waste any or cry if you spill it.*
> **Male, Muslim, aged 12**

> *The best thing you can do in life is be loving and trustworthy to others and to never be greedy or full of hatred.*
> **Male, Muslim, aged 12**

> *I think the best way to live is to accept people as they are. Respect and love others no matter what their colour, culture and age.*
> **Female, Muslim, aged 14**

> *If people want to live peacefully with the surrounding society, pray and think well of others who will end up devoted to you.*
> **Muslim, Female, aged 15**